Writing Women's History...
starting with your mother

Published by Mothership Stories Society 2018

New Westminster, Canada

Cover and design: Visnja Milidragovic

Printer: Lightning Source

Norry, Marilyn, 1957-, author

      Writing Women's History...starting with your mother / Marilyn Norry.

ISBN 978-0-9879844-2-5 (pbk)

      1. women's studies 2. memoir 3. history 4. writing manuals

The publisher is not responsible for websites and their content unless they are owned by the publisher.

To Jean Marie (Davis) Norry

1930-2018

Other books by Marilyn Norry (editor):

My Mother's Story: the originals Mothership Stories Society 2012

My Mother's Story: North Vancouver Mothership Stories Society 2012

VISIT US AT:

mymothersstory.org

Mothership Stories Society

#302-60 Richmond Street

New Westminster, B.C.

V3L 5R7

Writing Women's History...
starting with your mother

Marilyn Norry

MOTHERSHIP
STORIES SOCIETY

Writer's Declaration

This is to declare that I see you.
I know something of what it has cost you to be here.
I know the rewards that have come from what you have done
I acknowledge the pain that came from what you attempted to do
or what was done to you.

I am here to honor you by being your witness.

TABLE OF CONTENTS

Until the lion learns to write, every story glorifies the hunter.

African proverb.

Part 1

THE CHALLENGE

Write women into history and find a new freedom for yourself.

How?

Write the 2,000-word story of your mother's life, from beginning to end, just the facts, where you are just one of the facts. That's it!

Why?

Because in this time of great change the world needs to know how women lived through other times of great change. Because if you don't write it, your mother will likely be forgotten, as most women throughout history have been forgotten. Because once you tell her story, you are free to truly tell your own. Because it's time.

*D*espite its name, this project is not about mothering, good, bad or indifferent. It is an attempt to collect women's history before it slips away while freeing us from the unexamined ideas and experiences that tightly bind us to the archetypal idea of "mother." It's about sitting down for a few hours to shift our perspective from seeing our mothers only as caregivers to seeing them and all women as human beings navigating a challenging world. It's about uncovering all the great stories we have within us in which women are heroes as well as supporting characters.

MAKING THE SHIFT

All it takes is a story, the story you write of the facts of your mother's life. In writing this story, you will discover things about yourself, your mother, and your family that perhaps you never knew before. This simple act will shine a light on a life that might otherwise be forgotten by everyone but you and make it part of a larger story of what it was like to have been a human being in the 20th century. In writing it, you'll also be declaring that women have an indelible space in our collective history, in our current consciousness and in the future of humanity. You might feel a bit overwhelmed to be part of something so large but remember: you're in charge of the story you write. You can write for yourself, for your family, for your community or for the world. You decide.

This book will help you map your path and process, ease the way, answer questions and provide encouragement. If you wish, it will help you edit and share stories with your friends and perhaps even with the world, through our online My Mother's Story archive.

I don't know who you are. I don't know how old you are, what race or religion you are, where in the world you're living, or what has happened to bring you to the time and place where you're reading this book. But I do know a few things about your mother. She had a mother and a father, whom she may or may not have known, and was born sometime in the 20th century, somewhere on Earth, in a place with its own history and culture. She learned from the people around her how to make a living and get along with others. She met your father and had you. Maybe she wanted you; maybe she wasn't sure; maybe she was thinking of something else when you were born. She kept her wits and survived in the best way she could, making decisions that seemed right at the time.

Wherever she lived, the world was changing outside her window. Your mother lived a life of great value; she lived a great story. It's up to you to make it part of a written historical record, to give her life and story a voice.

CHANGING THE RULES

The world is changing. It's often hard to believe, but just a few generations ago, most women in the world were not formally educated. They were considered the responsibility and often the property of their fathers, brothers or husbands and were actively discouraged from speaking in public. Dying in childbirth was a common occurrence.

Well, we all know what's happened since. In the past century, many women around the world have been educated and have gained political, economic and reproductive freedoms. This has never happened before. Elizabeth Gilbert, the mega-selling author of *Eat Pray Love* and *Big Magic,* described our current era as "a vast and enormously historically unprecedented social history experiment." Regardless of what you think about this experiment, whether you're exhilarated or afraid, we're all in it together, trying to figure out what to do.

No one knows what will happen next. The rules of life—how we're supposed to live, the rules mothers have taught their children from the beginning of time—are changing. The rules that have governed Western societies are merging with those of other faiths and cultures, even as more women step forward into public roles.

Who is writing these new rules? The loudest among us? Politicians? Religious leaders? The market?

Wouldn't you like to have a say?

This project is not asking for your opinions and rhetoric, although they're probably fascinating, but rather evidence of how different rules played out in one person's life. How effective were the rules you grew up with, the ones your mother taught you? How effective were they for her? On what are we going to base the new rules? On how women have lived in the past? Or on how they want to live in the future? What do we actually know of other women's lives? What do we know of how women coped, or thrived or failed throughout history?

In 43 BCE, the Greek philosopher Cicero said, "Not to know what has been transacted in former times is to be always a child. If no use is made of the labours of past ages, the world must remain always in the infancy of knowledge." Men's history has been profusely recorded, but not women's. There is still a socially enforced fog of silence around most women's stories, a taboo against revealing any of the facts of their lives. Perhaps in the past it was believed women should be "protected" from the harsh scrutiny of public life but today women are still facing overt or unconscious bias against telling their stories. If you doubt this, look at the often vicious comments made on any woman's blog post, the slights made against women who have achieved extraordinary honours, how women are still edited out of historic photos or films as if they never existed. There are a lot of people who still want women to shut up and or disappear. Look at your own hesitation to publically bear witness to your mother.

In all cultures, there are books, sacred texts, commercials and scientific reports extolling what women should do, can't do, couldn't do. Isn't it time we collectively really looked at what women have done so the human race can finally, fully grow up?

The rules are changing, and we'll need the wisdom of all cultures, all races and all genders to find the best way to go forward.

Writing our mothers' stories following the guidelines of this writing recipe allows us to see individual lives from beginning to end; to see what choices our mothers believed they had, how fate intervened, and the consequences of their actions. We see their values in action. We also witness how character is revealed over the passage of time and perhaps discover moments of redemption. These are the elements of good storytelling.

Whether their mother told stories or remained silent on her life, many people who have written their mother's story report that they were able to see their mom—often for the first time—as a completely unique human being who participated fully in her time in history. She was much more than the socially held view that mothers be passive caregivers hidden away from public life.

Through the act of writing her life path, from wherever she was born to wherever we are now, we experience our mother's unique nature—and how we are all connected.

You can share your mother's story with others or keep it for yourself but, either way, you will be changed in writing it. You will break through any conscious or unconscious beliefs about mothers as perfect, mythically nurturing characters—or failures—to see all women as human beings. You will find your voice. You will also recognize the emotional journey taken by other people who have written about their mothers and appreciate their courage. You will experience how a woman can be the hero of her own story and hopefully see that you are the hero of yours.

If you do wish to make your story public, your mother's story will add to the ethnosphere, a word coined by ethnobotanist and anthropologist Wade Davis, the National Geographic Society's explorer in residence.

"We don't believe that polemics are persuasive or that politicians will lead the way," he explains. "But we do believe that storytelling can change the world."

He hopes that by hearing stories from other cultures, people will realize that "the world in which you were born is just one model of reality. These other cultures aren't failed attempts at being you; they are unique manifestations of the human spirit."

This is a distinction that needs to be expanded. The My Mother's Story project is evidence that we are all unique manifestations of the human spirit – your mother, you, the woman standing ahead of you in the grocery line, the people on TV. We may grow up thinking we're in competition with every-one—our siblings, neighbours, classmates, workmates, social systems, countries—and yet it becomes clear in reading mother stories that these interactions are merely the context everyone has to navigate on their own unique path. There is no normal, no ordinary. We are not all running in the same race and there are different finish lines. Women are not failed men. The American Dream is not the dream of everyone, including many Americans.

The woman standing ahead of you in the grocery line is living a different story than yours. You have each had to face different objectives, different circumstances. For the most part, it is a coincidence that your storylines are running parallel at this moment.

In writing your mother's story and reading the stories of others, you will see how more money has sometimes brought unhappiness; that sometimes getting fired is the best thing that happened to a person; that sometimes a brief life was the best life.

As we try to cope with the circumstances of our lives, reinvent ourselves and reframe our experiences in the face of adversity, many have found it helpful to experiment by reinterpreting their mother's life first.

This project is not about chronicling accomplishments. It's about telling the story. And each story is unique.

FINDING ROLE MODELS

By now you may be wondering who I am beyond My Mother's Story instigator and advocate. I'm a Vancouver actor you probably don't know who's been in many films and TV shows you probably do know. Like thousands of ordinary people engaged in the craft of acting, I'm not rich and famous. Over the past 30-odd years, I've had the good fortune to star in some plays and films, but mostly I play character or supporting roles, women (and some men) serving food, answering phones—girlfriends, best friends and mothers: loving mothers, crazy mothers and even a naked dancing zombie mother. I'm also a writer, director, producer and teacher and I work as an editor and dramaturg with playwrights and screenwriters, helping them clarify what they want to say and make their writing more effective.

I know stories; I love telling stories and listening to them. I love the speeches made at weddings. I remember lying under the kitchen table when I was little, hoping the grownups wouldn't notice me listening to their talk.

When I started the My Mother's Story project in 2004, I wanted to collect and share the stories of women's lives. My parents are avid genealogists, and my father is always saying, "We have the facts; we're not saving the stories!" Actors love playing characters who have complexity and depth, who beguile and confound other characters and the audience. There are many male characters like this but very few female ones. Were women that boring or were we just not telling their true stories?

Through this project, I have realized how much we take our own stories for granted, unaware how unique they are. This is especially true of women—our lives have rarely been recorded, and yet women have held civilizations together; have nurtured and taught generations of humans to look after one another. They've made dinner and made peace treaties; written grocery lists and code that enabled men to get to the moon; spied on Nazis and been Nazis; buried children and cured diseases. They've clothed families and created great (but usually underrated) literature and art.

How did they do this? How did they cope with the stress of their lives? What choices did they make?

I started My Mother's Story because I was bored with the way women were being portrayed in the media, especially women over 40. I was frustrated by the lack of history written about women. Where were our role models? Where were the women to inspire characters we could play?

My curiosity launched a project that has inspired hundreds of women and men to write their mothers' stories, and these stories reveal exciting, unique lives. Many of our mothers grew up in one world and died in another. They moved—across the street, across the country or across the world—survived wars inside and outside the home, got jobs, gave up jobs, had children, gave up children.

In the speech in which Elizabeth Gilbert described our world as a social experiment, she added that we have few role models of women who "did it all" because women like her grandmother had so few choices. Her belief was all the women around her grandmother lived the same life. My Mother's Story has made it clear that this idea—though understandable, given the lack of written history—is wrong, wrong, wrong. There are role models all around us! Women may have wanted to appear to be the same as their neighbours, and indeed for many their survival depended on fitting in, but they came from different backgrounds and lived very different lives. Few people know what someone else's mother lived through and accomplished against great odds because these stories have been secret. Inside their homes and outside in the world, women have lived lives that are absolutely unique—and their stories are all captivating.

IT'S TIME.

If you—

- believe women's history should be saved;

- want to learn how to write a good short story;

- want an easy way to organize material for writing memoir or biography;

- are looking for ideas for a film script, play or novel where women are the masters of their fate;

- want tips on writing an interesting, comprehensive genealogical story you can publish; or

- want your mother to be remembered, with all the happy and sad events of her life recorded—you will find what you need and how to accomplish it through this exercise.

Try it. Try it now, before the fearful part of your mind comes up with perfectly valid reasons why you don't have the time or energy, will or talent to begin. Aren't you curious to see what you'll discover? You can have a finished story in as little as two hours. Honest. But first you have to sit down.

THE RECIPE

Write the facts of your mother's life

from beginning to end

in less than 2000 words

where you're just a footnote.

When you're finished, and when you're ready,

read your story out loud to at least one person.

HOW THIS WORKS

This project is open to anyone with a mother. Your mother can be alive or passed on, adopted, alienated, beautiful, or difficult. Women and men can write of their mothers.

You are in charge. You don't need anyone's permission to write about your mother. As a courtesy it is recommended you read your story to your mother and other family in your story before sharing it with anyone else. It will start some wonderful conversations. If anyone disagrees with your story, hear them out. They may have new information, a different perspective or concerns that are easy to fix. However you are not writing the definitive story of your mother's life; this is your story of her.

If your mother doesn't want other people to know her story put it aside. She may change her mind; you may change your story. You have lots of time.

You decide how you want to use this book. It's filled with exercises and suggestions on how to tackle most issues. You can go back and forth, jump all over the place or read these pages in the order they're printed. All you need to do is ask "what do I need next?"

If you want to know more about the history of this project go to page 141.

Maybe you're one of those people who just needs to hear "Go!" and know what you want to say or are willing to discover as you go. If you feel ready to write your 2,000-word story right now, go ahead. You can find a suggested method for organizing your first draft, on page 120, or you can just launch now.

If you feel you need more time or direction, look at the exercises in Part 3 for suggestions on how to uncover memories, organize thoughts and build your confidence. The first section of exercises has questions that are relevant to writing your story following the recipe. The second section looks at your mother's culture, influences, home life and names.

Remember: this is your journey to become a storyteller. Maybe you'll try a few exercises, write a discovery draft, and then come back to see if there's an exercise or discussion that helps you answer questions you've discovered while writing. Maybe you'll want to do all the exercises, read all the discussion and then write. It's up to you. You may also find that an answer you give to a question or prompt becomes a spark for another story that calls to be written at another time.

If you have friends, neighbours or colleagues who have also undertaken to write and share their mothers' stories, the answers to these questions can be the basis for lively discussions. By figuring out how to articulate the rules and practices you grew up with, you open yourself up to seeing similarities and differences between your life and those around you. And you will find an appreciative audience for your writing and the stories you and your mother have lived.

WOMEN IN FILM — OR NOT

There are more and more articles in newspapers and on the internet about the disproportionate number of male and female characters in movies and television. Since we see women there all the time, it's hard for people not in The Biz to understand what the problem is. This "problem" is one of my chief motivations for starting this project.

In 1985 Alison Bechdel published a panel in her comic strip Dykes to Watch Out For, where a character presents a test for movie watching. It has become known as the Bechdel test. To pass this test, a film needs to:
- Have two or more female characters who have names;
- Who talk to each other;
- About something other than a man.

Less than a third of the films shown in any year in the US pass this test. This means there are women on screen, but they rarely talk to each other, and when they do they are mainly supporting a man who has the answers and solves all the problems.

Here's another perspective: Mick LaSalle, film critic at the San Francisco Chronicle, said in his book The Beauty of the Real that in 2001, of the 400 films distributed in the US, there were 19 female roles that were prominent enough that those who played them might be nominated for a best actress award. In 2010, there were 27, but that also included supporting roles.

In 2008, a female blogger (The Hathor Legacy) spilled the beans on why this situation keeps perpetuating: They're teaching it in film school. Her instructors informed her that if she wanted to see any of her work produced she had to stick with how the business worked:

According to Hollywood, if two women came on screen and started talking, the target male audience's brain would glaze over and assume the women were talking about nail polish or shoes or something that didn't pertain to the story. Only if they heard the name of a man in the story would they tune back in. By having women talk to each other about something other than men, I was "losing the audience".

Geena Davis, actor in Thelma and Louise and A League of Their Own, started the Institute on Gender in Media, which has sponsored research resulting in many kinds of statistics. One such report stated that cartoons and family films have crowd scenes that average out to being 17% female:

It wasn't the lack of female lead characters that first struck me about family films...It was the fact that the fictitious villages and jungles and kingdoms and interplanetary civilizations were nearly bereft of female population. This being the case, we are in effect enculturating kids from the very beginning to see women and girls as not taking up half of the space. Couldn't it be that the percentage of women in leadership positions in many areas of society—Congress, law partners, Fortune 500 board members, military officers, tenured professors and many more—stall out at around 17 percent because that's the ratio we've come to see as the norm?"

Through extensive research and testing the Institute discovered that, "The more hours of television a girl watches, the fewer options she thinks she has in life, and the more hours a boy watches, the more sexist his views become."

There is hope. What we see on TV and in movies have less to do with what scripts are written and how they are cast than with the deals that are made for financing and distribution. These aspects of the industry are managed by very few, very cautious people who mainly look at common factors of projects that have made money in the past. Recent statistical research has shown that, as of 2016, movies that passed the Bechdel Test have made more money that ones that didn't. With the financing and distribution of Oscar-nominated films like Hidden Numbers (chronicling the African-American women who worked as human computers on early NASA flights) a shift can be seen in the stories that are told on screens. Keep your eyes open for more.

Telling your mother's story means you are participating in this renaissance.

Jacques: All the world's a stage,

And all the men and women merely players;

They have their exits and their entrances,

And one man in his time plays many parts,

His acts being seven ages. At first the infant,

Mewling and puking in the nurse's arms.

Then the whining schoolboy, with his satchel

And shining morning face, creeping like snail

Unwillingly to school. And then the lover,

Sighing like furnace, with a woeful ballad

Made to his mistress' eyebrow. Then a soldier,

Full of strange oaths and bearded like the pard,

Jealous in honour, sudden and quick in quarrel,

Seeking the bubble reputation

Even in the cannon's mouth. And then the justice,

In fair round belly with good capon lined,

With eyes severe and beard of formal cut,

Full of wise saws and modern instances;

And so he plays his part. The sixth age shifts

Into the lean and slipper'd pantaloon

With spectacles on nose and pouch on side,

His youthful hose, well sav'd, a world too wide

For his shrunk shank, and his big manly voice,

Turning again toward childish treble, pipes

And whistles in his sound. Last scene of all,

That ends this strange eventful history,

Is second childishness, and mere oblivion,

Sans teeth, sans eyes, sans taste, sans everything.

William Shakespeare. As You Like It

Part II

THE ART OF STORYTELLING

WHAT DO YOU THINK WHEN YOU HEAR THE WORD "STORY"?
SOMETHING TOLD AROUND A CAMPFIRE OR TO A CHILD AT BEDTIME?
A CORPORATE OR POLITICAL MESSAGE? GOSSIP? A LIE?

In a classic sense, stories tell a sequence of events that involve change in a particular person or thing. How it was, what happened, how it is now. Beginning, middle, end. Sometimes they're fiction, sometimes they're true; they're often a mixture of both. "The names have been changed to protect the innocent." We tell stories to each other on social media, while washing dishes, while travelling and working, around the table during and after a meal. Some of these stories are accounts of the day while others are made up to entertain and/or educate listeners. Still others are histories of the family, tribe or race, passed on from generation to generation.

Stories are how we try to make sense of our world. Bits of information—events, relationships, words, objects, dreams—are arranged together to give meaning, perhaps point out a cause-and-effect relationship or provide an explanation. They establish order in the chaos of random events. When you see little kids watch the same video over and over or listen to the same bedtime story over and over, you can almost see neural pathways being created, a grid in their minds upon which all subsequent learning will be placed. This grid is a map we each have for "How Life Works."

Today corporate people say, "Tell us your story," as if that's something everyone knows how to do. For many of us trained to write resumes or think in terms of eulogies, this kind of disclosure seems self-aggrandizing and painful to consider. Aren't the rich and famous the only ones with stories? Often it seems unfair that after spending a life hiding facts about ourselves (everything that got us bullied or might have made us look peculiar or different) we are now supposed to declare these points with pride? How can people taught to think in terms of accomplishments suddenly shift to disclose personal relationships, background, failures and dreams? And yet the stories of our lives are what plays, movies, novels and campfires are all about. They allow us to connect with others.

FAMILY STORIES

Many First Nation tribes in North America did not hold a concept of private ownership for anything except stories. They were and are owned by wisdom keepers who are trained to repeat them exactly. Many of these stories deal with the consequences of greed but also tell the history of their people. The wisdom keepers could not improvise or rewrite or interpret or modify stories when they repeated them. Without written language, the sacredness of these oral traditions was maintained through vigilance. So when people were slaughtered, whether through wars or illness, much more was destroyed than individuals. Whole histories and perspectives on the human condition were lost.

My parents grew up on farms without TV and had a steady diet of family stories. They can recite facts, relationships and snippets of lives over 200 years old. I grew up "in town"; I know the plots of television shows; I remember little of the stories they told me. They get excited over the detective work of adding another relative to our family tree. I plead, "Can't we please talk about people who are alive?" I love the stories they tell, but unless they're written down there's no chance I will remember anything; my brain is already full, and my life seems to demand I cram in facts more pertinent to the present and future.

In the "old world" people told stories of how things were, of who we are, who our relatives are, where we've come from. In the "new world," we don't listen. We passively watch TV or the internet to learn about social behaviour; we get the "facts" from strangers. Anecdotal evidence, as any good scientist knows, is worthless, right?

We can see family stories given less and less value. Will the future be a dull grey of conformity as we all try to be like one another or like the characters on TV? In holding onto beliefs that say, "I'm nothing special," or, "No one would believe what happened," or, "The past is the past, and it's over," we perpetuate the feeling of our own insignificance. Our society may train us to be cogs in the system, to hold value for ourselves only as good citizens, consumers and caregivers, but we still have the option to see ourselves and our families as unique cogs. Spiritual cogs. Cogs that shine. It is in giving value to the unique colour of our lives that we will be part of an even more glorious global tapestry.

So how can we change the course of this attrition of meaning?

By telling our stories to our families and sharing them with the next generation before they're forgotten forever.

THE STORIES OF OUR LIVES

As humans we live both the inside and the outside of a story. We live our lives navigating the path ahead, looking forward, avoiding disaster, trying to accomplish our list of things to do, following goals, hoping for more, fearing loss or worse. We compare ourselves to others—friends, family and those on TV, and more often than not don't measure up. Doesn't it sometimes seem that reflections on those larger, personal issues (where am I going? What do I want?) only happen in crisis or while waiting for the traffic light to change, for the kettle to boil, or before starting sit-ups at the gym?

Modern therapies ask us to consider the stories we are living and the stories we tell ourselves. Think of this as the difference between plot and theme. Plot is the action that happens; theme is the meaning we give for why these events happened. A plot can have many themes. Every drunk has a sad story of what happened that now justifies their drinking. If they get sober, they change the way they look at the facts of their lives to give a different perspective or meaning.

Storytellers, those people who like telling stories at family gatherings, on stage, in books, plays, screenplays, songs or comic monologues, are always looking at their lives and the lives of friends and family for new material. In fact, they're often finding themes, frames and good lines for a story while they are living it! This detachment, taking one step back from the action and the arguments flowing around, can be infuriating to the other people involved ("Listen to me!"). But, besides providing useful material, it gives the storyteller a feeling of establishing order in often chaotic circumstances. We look at life from different angles, asking, "How can I talk about this later?" and "Where's the joke here?"

I remember one particularly hellish Christmas when I consciously decided I would survive only through living by two principles: Don't take anything personally; and, regardless what happens, it will turn out for the best. These became my themes and coloured the choices I made (or didn't make) as I lived from moment to moment. Through disaster after disaster (and believe me there were a few!) I thought about the sentence structure I would use when I wrote this story down, wondering, at times with panicked amusement, what could possibly happen next? I survived, we all survived, and it made a great story.

MOTHER'S STORIES

Perhaps your mother was a storyteller. Some people can't wait to get the vivid pictures their mother told them about her life down on paper. These are the stories that flow, that come ready-made with structure, details, punchlines and even the musical vocal cadence for how they're told. If this is your experience, rejoice! You have been steeped in story and know how rich it makes your life.

People with this wealth still have work to do. One of their challenges is to decide which of their mothers' many stories to include in their 2,000 words. A subtler challenge is to see the woman who experienced these adventures rather than just what she saw. And a finer challenge still comes from having to craft the stories of her life where she didn't provide a frame. These are the events they witnessed that have not yet been made into stories—perhaps her despair or her aging and lastly her death. Many have felt intimidated about putting their reflections alongside the stories of a master—yet this is their story of their mother, not just of the stories she told.

Then there are those of us who have to craft stories from silence. Our mothers didn't talk about their lives, or we didn't listen. Maybe she died a long time ago or thought all stories were gossip or too painful to tell. Fear not! This book was also created for you! You have a story to tell even if it's the story of why you don't have a story.

WHEN IT'S TIME TO TELL

Remember you are writing this story first for yourself; then you can decide who else will see it. Remember that it's often easier to tell a story long after it's happened, when the arc can be more clearly seen, and the pain of events has softened.

If your mother is alive and refused to talk earlier in her life, it could be that she's open now to discussing what happened. Asking specific questions will always get better results than, "Tell me about the war," or similarly vague requests. Once you have written what you know, you will know more specifically what to ask her.

Many of the people whose mothers have died say that they resisted starting this project lest the grief they felt at her passing overwhelm them again. They didn't want to open that file. So, they said they couldn't remember anything. When prompted to write (or pushed as I did to some in the early days) they discovered that writing what they knew started a flow of memories that opened the door to more. They realized they were now ready to talk to relatives and friends, to find out answers to questions they were afraid to ask earlier.

My father wrote his mother's story when he was 85. His relationship with her was the most profound one of his life even though (or perhaps because) she died when he was five years old. He wrote her story following the recipe with details so fresh it was like he had been writing them in his head his whole life. Actually, I really think that was what he did. Once it was on paper, though, he found he didn't have to keep poking that wound in his heart; he still missed her, but she lived on through the story he'd told.

THE POWER OF STORYTELLING

This is the power of storytelling. Life and order are breathed into memories, ideas, and images so they exist as a whole thing separate from us rather than fragments scattered inside our heads. Like baking a cake, we mix the ingredients together, let them sit somewhere hot and then stand back to see how all the elements have come together. The kind of story we want depends on whom we imagine telling this story to: our children, our grandchildren, our friends, our mother, the world. Different audiences want to hear different details but the facts remain the same. Once you have pondered and sifted through the facts, figured out what's important to you, and figured out how to talk about the painful parts, you will know how to tell this story to anyone. The Italians have a term for it: *sprezzatura*—carefully contrived spontaneity.

WRITING A DISCOVERY DRAFT

Telling a story needn't be difficult; it needn't be scary, take up loads of time or inflict heartache. We tell stories all the time but often we don't know the point of our stories until we're finished. "Aha!" we finally say while our audience breathes a sigh of relief. "That's what I was trying to get at!" Sometimes we call this thinking out loud. There's a niggling thought, a new perspective, an unfinished important idea that keeps us talking and talking until we figure out a way to fully articulate it.

It's the same with writing but quieter. We write and write and write through the layers of thoughts in our brains trying to get to the crux of what's important. Regardless of the form it takes—story, script, poem, prospectus, email, love letter—the first draft of writing is a discovery draft where you write to find out what you want to say. This is a fact that inexperienced writers don't believe: it's very rare that a work comes out of someone's head onto the page fully formed and perfect.

The writing recipe used here establishes a form that you fill with your memories, each pulling you towards the next event in the sequence of a life. Have faith that the facts you tell will be interesting enough that you needn't worry about making your writing interesting. There's no need to fabricate or embellish.

THIS IS YOUR ART.

A friend of mine was diagnosed with HIV in 1986. He's in his 70s now, has buried many friends and lovers and faced his own death many times. It's been a painful, often bitter road. Years ago, I remember him saying, "The only point to experiencing pain is to put it in your art."

What is your art? Beyond what we call the Fine Arts—music, dance, painting, sculpture, writing, film, theatre—there's the art of medicine, the art of conversation. Anything you're good at—that thing where you've always had an instinctive feel for how parts go together or what to do next—is likely your art. Your intuition is engaged in this act as well as your thoughts and feelings.

There is a difference between something created technically and something that embodies art. You experience this in the difference between the work of a cook and a chef, or, if you were lucky, between a restaurant and your mother's cooking. Even if they're using the same recipe, the food prepared by a chef (or your mother) has a magic cohesion, a splendour in the mouth that's more than just food. Art can find its way into anyone's cooking, but an artist finds a way to more consistently transcend the ordinary in their work. For centuries there have been arguments over what qualifies as art in the worlds of food, paintings, music, literature and theatre. Suffice it to say that something is defined as art when the impact is bigger than the product. When a product is created with art, it's not so much a thing as the embodiment of a dialogue between an artist and the world.

Do you remember being affected by a poem or painting, a dance or piece of music? Any meaning that came to you was the result of many technical elements coming together to convey something else—a moment of understanding, acceptance of mystery or a perturbing question on the human condition. You are an artist when you step outside a situation or question and open your heart to see it from a different angle. An artist looks for unexpected patterns—of beauty, absurdity, pathos and joy—but also patterns of similarity and difference. An artist frames physical reality to create connection.

The story you write following this recipe will allow for that connection. The story is not you; it is not your mother. It is art. It can hold the pain, laughter, mystery, and the truth of the life you've witnessed or discovered. It will allow you to detach from your memories and experiences to craft and ponder them objectively. This will happen because this recipe just happens to embody the essential elements of good storytelling.

...AND ART REQUIRES DISCIPLINE

A sonnet is a poem of fourteen lines with ten syllables per line.

Haiku is a poem of seventeen syllables used in three lines of five, seven, five.

A limerick is usually a bawdy poem of five lines where the first two lines rhyme, the second two shorter lines rhyme, and the last line rhymes with the first. AABBA.

Poets for centuries have challenged themselves to fit profound or witty ideas into these tight constructs and admiration comes from how effective they are able to say what they want to say despite the restrictions. In fact the restrictions add to the fun.

What's the difference between journal writing and a story? Journal writing has transient meaning and thus never needs to end; stories have intentional meaning that is conveyed because they come to an end. Writing in a journal is writing; writing a story is art.

You may find a meaning for your mother's story in your first pass discovery draft; you may decide to use more craft and write another draft for a different meaning or for a different audience. The discipline of creating art is finding objectivity to your subject and knowing when it's finished.

● ●

This book will take you through the process of opening to and discovering the stories stored within you. The recipe enforces the discipline of structure but you will breathe life and meaning into the stories you write.

WRITING ABOUT OUR MOTHERS

Trying to be objective about your mother is a weird but interesting assignment. I suspect there's so much power in these stories because this kind of objectivity is so unexpected.

Writing about your mother in this way is rather like being the tour guide of a place you know. All you can do is show people the sights—the beauty, the raw bits, the grandeur—and hope that they get it, hope that they see the whole experience through your eyes and heart.

The story you write following this recipe is more like a movie or play than a novel. In a novel, the writer can say what's going on in the minds of their characters. They can have opinions; they can write on and on about anything they like with perhaps only a slight connection to the story they're telling. A novel can be 100 pages long or 3,000 or 7,312 (according to Mental Floss, the longest novel ever). A play or movie script has more restrictions: the story is usually told in about 100 pages, and it stays focused on the plot rather than taking digressions. As actors, we're trained to see that our characters are revealed only by what they say, what they do and what others say about them. Costume designers add to this through how the character looks and dresses; set designers add the context of the character's home or environment. These elements are also in your story. Just the facts.

Everyone can write a good story. We tell stories all the time! Even if you don't consider yourself a writer you've seen movies and know how they unfold—the star does this and then this happens and then, and then and then. There's no need for your story to be fancier than that.

The effectiveness of your story is in what you're saying, not how you're saying it. In fact, it's better if it sounds like it's told in your voice, the way you would tell the story out loud. Writing it, however, gives you the opportunity to decide what the important moments of your mother's life might be and to work through the difficult parts of her life; figuring them out, like an artist, to see them from a different angle. Once you've done this, you can tell the story out loud to anyone. And you will have experienced what it takes to write a good story.

• •

RULES OF GOOD WRITING

I've collected rules on the craft of writing from lists made by various writers—writers like Kurt Vonnegut, John Steinbeck, Neil Gaiman, and Pixar. The writing recipe of My Mother's Story limits your options but also forces you to use these rules and see why they're important.

1. Find a subject you care about.
   Even if you didn't know your mother or even if you didn't like her, how your mother is portrayed is something everyone cares about. It's personal. Caring means your heart is engaged, which engages your intuition; this is what you need to be an artist with your words. It's amazing how many people start writing projects from an intellectual standpoint. They work on stories that are "a good idea," and then wonder why they get bored in the middle, or quit, or their readers get bored, and there are no sales. If you don't care, or are afraid to care, no one else will care either. You will have a hard time editing or crafting a better story when you have no personal stake in your subject.

2. Keep it simple.
   Sometimes people get so wound up (and their stories get so convoluted) when they don't trust their material to hold the interest of the reader. Simple is interesting. Simple structure, simple language. The hard work was living this story; all you need to do is write it down.

3. Sound like yourself.
   If you didn't trust me when I said it, well, Kurt Vonnegut says the same thing. You have a lovely voice; use it.

4. Focus on the interesting.

This is important advice for writing in general and especially for this assignment. All too often we trap ourselves into a perspective that enforces the ordinary and the mundane, especially when describing our mothers. Contrary to the rules of the school ground where everyone tries to fit in, life is made sweeter and writing more delicious by emphasizing the unique details of a person or scene.

5. In writing, your audience is one single reader.

If you're feeling self-conscious about your words, it could be you're trying to please too many people—an editor, your mother, your friends, a critic. Well, of course you'll feel blocked! Imagine telling this story to one person. Who would you best like to know your mother? Who would most appreciate your mother's unique story? It might be a friend, your child; it may be someone you make up. One of the writers wrote her story to an imaginary woman in Italy whom she was sure would like her mom if only she knew her. Some have written their stories as letters to me or someone else. Focus from your heart. Once you have completed your discovery draft, you can see how it might be modified again for your children or a friend and you can write a version for them.

6. Write freely and as rapidly as possible and throw the whole thing on paper. Never correct or rewrite until the whole thing is down.

Writers with loads of talent and years of experience know how easy it is to lose a train of thought, become self-conscious or get stuck looking for the right word or phrase. What every writer wants is to find themselves lost in a flow of words that appear on the page as if by magic. They know that the words they write might not be in the final copy, but the trick is to get out of the way of this flow. Write anything, just write. Write fast, even if it's garbage. Gone are the days when paper and ink were expensive, when correcting mistakes meant retyping every single word and letter again and again. There is no cost now to fixing later. Get it down. Perfect doesn't come from your head; it is crafted on the page later.

7. Fail early; fail often.

Accessing intuition means allowing for half-baked ideas and glimmering thoughts; ideas you'd respond to with, "I don't even know what this means," will pop into your mind with equal weight to your most brilliant impulses. Few people can tell the difference until they're written down. Don't be afraid of writing stupid ideas; in fact, embrace them. Jump. Try something new. Fly. Maybe crash. Learn, try again. Writing everything that comes to mind is rather like painting the bathroom, with a lot less cleanup. If it doesn't work, well, it's a small room and easy to paint again. Try to put aside any worries about what people will think of the final product—you're not there yet! Know that eventually you will have an interesting story that works. Your mother already did the hard work living it. All you have to do is give the report.

8. If a scene or a section gets the better of you and you still think you want it—bypass it and go on.

This is an especially important rule in writing memoir or biography. There are moments in any life that are hard to live, let alone write about. Don't give up on the rest of the story because of these moments; just skip over them and keep going! They're like sculptures that sometimes sit in the middle or to one side of a road; they may be huge or small but the road still continues past them to its destination. Write the road, then come back and give these moments the artistic attention they deserve. There's a section called Dealing with Scary Stuff with suggestions on how to deal with many of these issues, later in the book on page 83.

9. Don't tell. Show.

This is on everyone's "Best Advice to Writers" list. If you know your mother had a sense of humour, write a joke she told and the reaction she got. If she loved singing, write of an event when she sang or about what she liked to sing. Who was her favourite singer? Get specific, so we can see and smell and taste the world she inhabited. See how many of the five senses you can include in your story.

10. You admire a character more for trying than for their successes.

We grant fictitious characters the right to fail and learn but rarely allow this for the living. Get the idea of accomplishments out of your head. Did your mother pour her heart into something that ultimately didn't work out? What was her reaction to this "failure"? Now is your chance to record the full story. Readers empathize with and understand people who struggle.

11. The adverb is not your friend.

In the section on editing I'll get into this more but suffice to say adverbs indicate you don't trust your work and you think you need to be fancy. They clutter a story and you don't need them.

12. Laugh at your own jokes.

Allow yourself to be delighted in your work. If you laugh, your reader will laugh; if you cry, your reader will cry. This rule is also a reminder to mix up the content of your story so there is humour. Too often people get into a "tragedy voice" or a "just the facts" voice and forget their mother also laughed occasionally. This is especially true if there's a real tragedy in your mother's life. Find some lightness and humour elsewhere to balance it.

13. Pity the Reader.

Readers have enough to do figuring out how little marks and ticks on a page could actually be words with meaning. It behooves us to remember (and take great joy in being able to use words like behooves) that our readers need simplicity and clarity just to understand what we're saying. Give them enough names and dates that they can keep up and not so many that they're confused. Exercise good taste. Gruesome details that further the story, like the list of medical conditions one woman's hypochondriac mother apparently suffered, are acceptable; discussions of your mother's prolapsed uterus are more about you wanting to shock than pity your readers.

14. Read your work out loud.

All the great writers do this. It gets your writing out of your head to where you can hear it in the world. Hearing your words gives you a visceral response to them, allowing you to feel as well as think your meaning, and to get a sense of what your readers might experience. Have you used the best word? Be a poet. Be inventive. Shakespeare made up words that had the sound he wanted and then he gave them a meaning. Auspicious, sanctimonious, clangor and dwindle are some of the words Shakespeare made up. Reading out loud allows you to hear the rhythm of your sentences. You are writing music as well as words. Roy Peter Clark gives an example of this in his book *Writing Tools*:

> *This sentence has five words. Here are five more words. Five-word sentences are fine. But several together become monotonous. Listen to what is happening. The writing is getting boring. The sound of it drones. It's like a stuck record. The ear demands some variety.*
>
> *Now listen. I vary the sentence length, and I create music. Music. The writing sings. It has a pleasant rhythm, a lilt, a harmony. I use short sentences. And I use sentences of medium length. And sometimes,*

when I am certain the reader is rested, I will engage him with a sentence of considerable length, a sentence that burns with energy and builds with all the impetus of a crescendo, the roll of the drums, the crash of the cymbals—sounds that say listen to this, it is important.

15. Put it aside.

Read it pretending you've never read it before. Show it to friends whose opinion you respect and who like this kind of thing. Part of the recipe: the process of writing your mother's story is completed when you read it out loud to one person. Choose this person carefully—someone who can listen without judgment. And if your mother is still alive, read it to her when you're ready.

16. Trying for theme is important, but you won't see what the story is actually about until you're near the end of it.

There's no need to be clever all at once, to prove you can be perfect in one try. Allow yourself the possibility of discovery, the joy of not knowing everything. The theme is what you'll write for others. As an artist, you must write for yourself first—the discovery draft is yours. This is why I recommend you just splat your words on the page as fast as possible. If you try for a theme too soon or impose a literary construct on your work, chances are your words will be plastic and stiff and you'll miss the chance to surprise yourself. Write what happened first and then see what of that you want to keep.

In the Hebrew Bible, the sixth of the Ten Commandments brought down the mountain by Moses is 'Honour your mother and father'. Many people throughout history have felt this guilt-inducing commandment the hardest to keep. What does it even mean today? Love? Approval? What if, to quote Rabbi Angela Buchdahl, this means, "to make peace with who our parents really are"?

Part III

MAPPING A LIFE

MOST PEOPLE IN THE WORLD, REGARDLESS WHEN OR WHERE THEY GREW UP, THINK OF THEIR MOTHERS AS PERFECT OR FAILED CAREGIVERS, SOMEONE WHOSE SOLE PURPOSE WAS TO BE A MOTHER TO THEM. IT TAKES A SHIFT OF AWARENESS TO SEE HER AS A WOMAN WITH HOPES AND DREAMS, TO SEE THE WORLD THROUGH HER EYES.

THE QUESTIONS IN THIS SECTION WILL HELP YOU MAKE THAT SHIFT. YOU WILL ANSWER SOME WITH ONE WORD, OTHERS WITH ESSAYS; SOME ANSWERS YOU'LL KNOW RIGHT AWAY, OTHERS WILL COME AFTER LONG PONDERING, AND STILL OTHERS WILL REMAIN PART OF THE MYSTERY OF THE WOMAN WHO WAS YOUR MOTHER.

Challenge your assumptions. Look beyond the cloud of feelings you hold about this woman. Try to see her in a new light as you shift from child to storyteller, from writer to historian. When I started this project, I sent out an email with the writing recipe and said, "Go!" Some people were able to write their stories from that directive; others needed to warm up to the idea, listen to stories and discussions, think about what they wanted to say, write a few drafts and eventually get down on paper what they really wanted to say.

When I started leading workshops on this project, I came up with writing prompts and questions that covered much of what we in the original group discovered in our discussions to be the journey we had taken to write our stories. This book has expanded that journey even more. These many exercises are given in the hope that everyone reading this can find a path where their fears are allayed, their questions are answered and they're able to sit down to write their mother's story.

INVITING THE MUSE

In Greek mythology Zeus, the father of the Gods, sired nine daughters with Mnemosyne, the Titan goddess of memory, to celebrate victory of the Olympian gods over the Titans. These daughters, or muses, were created to help people forget the evils of the world. Each of them looked after a different art or science.

Calliope presides over justice, epic poetry, music and writing.

Clio is the protector of history.

Erato is the protector of lyrical and love poetry.

Euterpe is the protector of song and poetry of death, love, and war..

Melpomene is the protector of tragedies and created the art of rhetoric.

Polyhymnia is the protector of divine hymns. She also created geometry and grammar.

Terpsichore is the protector of dance and education.

Thalia is the protector of comedy, the sciences (geometry, architecture, agriculture) and symposiums.

Urania is the protector of celestial bodies and created astronomy.

It was the practice of the ancient Greeks (and many people since) to call upon a muse whenever they attempted an artistic creation. The muse offered her wisdom and a feeling of rightness which we now call intuition.

In looking over this list of specialties it seems fitting that we call upon these feminine muses for help when writing about our mothers. Memories, history, poetry, grammar—call on any or all that apply to where you need support right now. Or call upon your own gods or familiars. Or your mother. Or just breathe deeply and open yourself to listening for what needs to be said.

This project of writing about your mother involves both the right and the left side of the brain: on the one hand there are the facts, the rational structured story you put together; on the other hand there are all those emotions. Trying to do this with only the left side of your brain will give you a list of dry facts; trying to write from your right side could very well leave you overwhelmed with emotions that cause you to quit. So think of "relaxing with a muse" as bridging the two parts of yourself. Or to put it another way, your impulse will move from subconscious understanding, to conscious imagining, and finally to articulated story.

Asking for help, or opening to inspiration, allows you to use both sides of your brain together and write your story your own way and in your own time. It may take some time to feel ready. Rather than beating yourself up with psychological rationalizations or justifications for procrastination or fear you can simply say "I'm waiting for the muse."

• •

What is your usual practice when getting ready to write? Make lists? Meditate? Clean the house? Do you make an appointment to work on a schedule or do you prefer to be caught by inspiration and write in little bursts? Every writer has a different method that they swear by, often including lucky hats, rocks, photos, music, coffee routines, or pens that have proven to attract inspiration. Sometimes different projects have demanded different props and rituals. We are not so different than the Greeks. How you prepare is up to you. All this is to say trust your instincts.

However, beware of the notion that writing is a hifalutin act that requires the right time, the right place, the right lighting, silence, perfumed air or any other external trappings. You can write anywhere and at any time. And when the muse arrives with a stream of thoughts and sentences that fill you to bursting, respond right then and there and write. She is fickle and may not soon come back.

In her book of essays, *Dancing At The Edge of the World,* Ursula Le Guin captures the image of a woman standing by a table heaped with laundry all shoved aside as she feverishly writes sentence after sentence on scraps of paper. This is also what creativity can look like. Remember: by following the writing recipe, you can splat down the facts you know of your mother's life, your discovery draft, in two hours.

Ready?

Get yourself a notebook, some scrap paper, a new file in your computer—whatever lets you be comfortable, creative and committed today. Sharpen your pencils. Fill your pen (does anyone fill pens anymore?)

This is where you'll answer the questions asked here. You can also draw or doodle, paint, paste photos or flowers—whatever you need to activate your memory and get your fingers tapping or pen moving. The story of your mother needs lots of primordial soup to rise out of. You can use the answers you've written here in your story or they can be used as writing prompts or meditations. All the information you record or consider will be valuable.

The first set of exercises record the facts as you know them. The next set is where you can discover broad reflections on your mother and her world. While answering either set think in terms of stories you could tell; think of events that happened and write them down.

WRITING THE WOOD

Writing a story is like building a house. You see a need; you create a design; you gather materials and then put them together. Except with a story, you have to write your materials; you have to write the wood before you can build. And sometimes you don't use all the materials you've gathered. Sometimes the materials you gather will change your design.

Writing memoir and biography is easy in one way because unlike fiction, you already have the sequence of events you need to record—someone has already lived them! But in writing about our mothers, many people discover that things they've believed all their lives end up being wrong. Some people assume they don't know anything because their mother died or left a long time ago, but, through writing, realize they actually know a lot. Others have the sobering realization they forgot to ask questions of the person who lived so close to them, who had such an influence on their lives. But all is not lost! Even in this case, the mind holds onto many trivial facts forever. Write what you know. As one memory rises in your mind to be recorded on paper, another deeper memory will rise to take its place.

You may imagine the story of your mother's life would have the literary equivalent of a curved staircase as a central motif and then discover the facts lend themselves to a one-floor rancher. Or perhaps you know your mother as a humble woman and discover her story is much more exotic, much richer than imagined, like a Southern plantation mansion with big columns out front. Regardless what you think of your mother before you start writing, the facts of her life will open new vistas for you.

The stories of our families sometimes flow around and through us so fast we don't know they're there or can't repeat them until we experience a trigger that lets loose a barrage of memory. Often, they don't seem interesting or epic or important enough to be remembered, except for maybe what Grandpa said that day when he was drunk. But whether you liked Grandpa or not or believed him or not, these are the stories that make up your perception of how the world works. They lurk unseen, unprocessed until brought forth. That's what we're doing here. And, after writing answers here, these events and perceptions can be compared with others making the world a richer place. Remember: some people know their mothers lived fascinating lives; other people discover this. Those are the only two possibilities.

EXERCISE: MIND SPARKS

These questions are memory prompts to get your brain focused on specifics. Answer quickly and don't worry if you don't have answers for some. Write down what first comes to mind and anything that jogs a story or image. Keep going!

Your mother's full name

Her birthdate

Her birthplace

Her parent's names

What was a unique/interesting/weird thing about where/how your mother grew up?

What was her favourite toy?

What did she look like as a child?

When your mother was a child, what did she dream of becoming as an adult?

Her parents—

is there anything unusual to note here?

Describe their appearance and temperament.

Describe their occupations.

How old were her parents when your mother was born?

What was her relationship like with her father?

What was her relationship like with her mother?

Her siblings

Name them in order if you can.

Who was her favourite?

Did she fight with any of her siblings?

What games did they play?

Her education

Name her elementary, high school, college, university or any other training and note its location.

Which classes did she enjoy?

Which classes did she hate?

What was the highest grade or level she finished?

Why did she leave school?

Did she have a best friend?   What adventures did they have?

What did they talk about?

Romance

How did she meet your father?

What year did this happen?   How old was she?   How old was he?

Did she have other romances? (Before, after, during?)

Did she have a wedding?   When was it?   What was it like?

Did she have a honeymoon?   If not, what did she do after the wedding?

Babies

List the names and birthdates of babies (including abortions and miscarriages, if known).

Did she like babies?

Did she stay home with her babies or work outside the home?

Her work

What jobs did she have as a teen?

What jobs did she have as an adult?

What jobs did she like?

Did she have jobs she hated?

Her Homes

As an adult, where did she live?

Describe her homes: split level, suburban, apartment, cabin, palace?

Who chose where she lived? Your mom? Dad? Someone else?

How did she decorate?

How did she clean?

Did she garden?

Was there a constant in all her homes, such as music, flowers or dirty dishes?

Food

What was her favourite food to eat?

What was her favourite food to make?

Was she a good cook?

What were her hobbies? If she had a spare minute, what would she do?

What was her favourite song?

Against what, or whom, was her greatest struggle?

What did she think was her greatest achievement?

What would the world consider her greatest achievement?

What was her greatest passion?

What was her greatest fear?

What was the bravest thing you remember her doing?

Is there a time when she "spoke her truth"? Where was she? What happened? What did she say?

What was her favourite joke? Describe her telling it.

Describe a moment when she laughed.

What is the funniest thing you remember her doing?

What scent did she wear?

What smell reminds you of her?

How did she dance?

Who were her role models?

When do you think she said "I love you" for the first time—to anyone?

How did your mother express love?

How did she express anger?

After her children left home, did she finally do things she'd always wanted to do or do something very different? What was it?

Thinking of her as a young girl, how do you think she was changed at the end of her life?

Where is your mother now?

If she has passed away, how did she die? What year?

How old were you when she died?

What event or fact of your mother's life is the hardest to talk about?

What is the biggest question you have about her now?

Are you surprised by any answers you've given here?

EXERCISE: TIMELINE

It's said that the most stressful times in a person's life are when they marry, have children, change jobs, change homes, or deal with the deaths of loved ones. Looking back at your life, you can see that these events are often markers against which other memories line up. "It was before we moved to Montgomery." "It was around the time my father died."

This exercise is to plot the markers of someone else's life—your mother's. Don't worry if you don't know some dates. You will probably have to look up others so keep this chart to fill in over time.

1930   1957   2018

Draw a line down the long side of a page. On one end, put the year of your mother's birth. At the other end put the year of her death or the present year.

In between, mark down the dates:

When you were born

When your siblings were born

When your mother married your father

When her mother died (if known)

When her father died (if known)

Dates of other important deaths—children, siblings, friends, husbands

Important moves

Important events—graduation, awards, trips, divorce, new job

Major illnesses, accidents and injuries: your mother's, her children's, her parents.

As you fill in this page, your memories of your mother will line up against these facts of her life. You may notice things like time clusters where a few major events happened at once. These would have been a times of great stress in your mother's life.

How did she cope?
Did she make any life changing decisions at these times of stress?

You may have to speculate. For example, many people consider changing their lives in some way when a parent dies. You may not remember when her parents died but these would have been big events for her.

How do we know the stories we know? When did we hear them?

Social etiquette in many cultures says that the stories we tell from the past should only be about good things. "If you can't say something nice about a person, don't say anything at all." Considering the atrocities of the past century, some may think this is still a good idea. Other people didn't tell stories at all, good or bad. Still other people had family who revelled in stories, entertaining one another with observations, constantly trying out new material or repeating well-worn reflections of their past.

These exercises will give you the opportunity to see the way you were raised and the stories told there as raw material for further storytelling. You will be detaching from and examining the context of your family as you would a play or movie or children's story: who are the characters? Where are they living? How are they distinct? How can they be easily described?

EXERCISE: STORYTELLING IN MY MOTHER'S FAMILY

Did your mom have one story she loved to tell or a period of her life she could describe in detail while ignoring other times? Or was she too busy, not interested, or too afraid to speak of her past? Perhaps when you asked for stories, she thought you were too young to hear the truth of her life. It happens: have you told your children the truth of your life yet?

What's your earliest memory of hearing stories of your family?

Who told you the stories of your mother's childhood?

Who is the person you remember telling the most stories of your family?

Describe a time you remember when they told a story. Make this description as rich as possible—the place, the date, who else was there and the story they told. Did their voice change when they told stories?

"What do you expect from a Johnson?" "We are the Staten Island Andersons." "You get that from your mother's side for sure." What will these statements mean when the stories behind them aren't remembered? Will it be a good thing or a bad thing if we wipe the slate clean of the insults, struggles, pain and laughter we grew up with? Are we the ones who get to choose what to forget or should we leave that decision to future generations?

We have learned much in the past century. Changing a name does not change a history. Not talking about it does not make the past go away. We cannot assume that family stories will be told by others, that they will magically exist forever. We are made of the stories of our ancestors. Today doctors ask for full family medical records; people test their DNA to find out their complete genetic history. Open adoptions have put to a lie the notion that birth parents and their history need to be kept secret from children. Transparency, accountability and full disclosure are concepts people are seeking in families as well as of corporations and governments.

What do we owe ourselves in terms of our family history? There is therapeutic value in telling the truth as we see it—of our childhoods and our family legacy—but there is also a great benefit in letting it go. What do we owe our children? What do we owe the world? These are questions only you can answer for yourself. As I've said before, write first; then decide who gets to know more.

A friend of mine took her husband's last name when she married because she liked the sound of it better than her own. His name was the last name of his mother's second husband, a man long deceased who had adopted her husband as a boy for a short while. Her husband's mother had since married twice more. So how much claim does my friend have on her name?

Genealogists have determined how to chart this flow of generations (it's not a new phenomenon), but last names are evolving, from identifiers almost to accessories. Not everyone named MacDonald is a Scot. What have last names ever meant for women? Ownership tags or sources of pride? Identifiers for legal contracts or for bloodlines? Women in Iran, China and other countries have never changed their names from their father's when they married. So their children and husbands have always had different surnames. In many Spanish-speaking countries, both mother's and father's surnames are used. Cher, Madonna, Beyoncé and Prince all became so famous they are known by only one name.

EXERCISE: MY MOTHER'S NAMES

What stories do you know of your last name? Some people could write a book on this (please do!) while others know next to nothing. Write what you know.

What three adjectives would you use to characterize this side of your family?

Do you have more information on your mother's family or your father's? Why?

There's no right answer. These are clues to the stories that lie hidden in your mind. Reasons might be:

- My father never talked about his family.
- We always visited Mom's side.
- Mom was the black sheep of her family, and they hated her.
- Dad's family didn't like Mom.
- There was a fight long ago, and people stopped talking.
- Everyone died a long time ago.
- It was too painful for Dad to talk about (or too painful for Mom).

Write what you know – the feuds, the fights, the failings, the glory.

What are the stories you know of your mother's maiden name? Her father's family?

Can you characterize this side of your family in three words?

What are the stories you know of your mother's, mother's last name? For some people this is a family with great history; for others, it has never been known.

How would you characterize this family in three words?

Which name did your mother identify with most? Her husband's? Her father's? Her mother's? Her grandmother's?

IMAGINING A LIFE

Writing the story of your mother's life requires you to step aside and let the spotlight shine on her not you. It requires you to link thoughts and memories that have been separate in your mind and see their relationship. By letting go of our cherished opinions we are able to imagine what it might have been like to see the world through her eyes. Sometimes what we see is a surprise; sometimes it contradicts what we believed to be true; sometimes there's a truth we'd rather not face. Use these exercises to write it all down and sort out later what you need and want.

VISUALIZATIONS

Telling the story of your life or of the life of someone else requires you to willingly create a space of introspection. In this case, though, rather than looking in, it means to step outside—to step outside a living story and see it as a static thing, a work of art. Like an artist, you need to detach, become objective and try to find "the big picture." This means placing your subject in the context of their time and place and remembering that even though you know what happens next, they didn't.

EXERCISE: VISUALIZATION 1
....

This exercise is part memory and part imagination. Read through the visualization and then, sitting with your eyes closed, imagine the images presented. You will write for 10 minutes at the end of this exercise so be aware of what you see. Don't worry if something doesn't make sense or isn't what you thought it would be. Be open to surprises.

What is today's date? Now, do some math: What year was it when you were five? (If age five was a traumatic time for you, pick another less stressful young age to remember.) Taking today's date, think of this day in that year.

Now, in your mind's eye, think of where you were living on that day. What city? What did your house look like? Imagine your kitchen.

It's this day of the year you are five and you're sitting in your kitchen having breakfast. Can you see the table? What are you eating? What are you wearing? Who else is in the room?

On this day in the year you are five, who else is living in your house? Which siblings? How old are they? Can you see them? Is there anyone who has not been born yet? Is Grandma or Grandpa there? Anyone else? Is your dad at home? If he isn't, where is he?

Now, even though she might not have been there on this day, imagine your mother standing by the counter. What's she doing? What's she wearing? How old is she? When you were five, how old was your mom? Do you have any feelings as you look at her there?

Now on this day in the year you are five, what is going on outside your house? In your neighbourhood? In your city? In the world?

You probably weren't aware of this when you were five but now, as an adult, you can add the greater world to your story. Did any of these events have an impact on your family? Did they have an impact on your breakfast?

Now looking at yourself again, you when you were five, know that this little girl doesn't know what's going to happen next, but you do. Give her a hug and tell her everything's going to be alright.

Now allow your brain and heart to come together. You're going to write for 10 minutes, capturing this moment from your past. You, your house, your mother. Keep writing even if you think it's garbage (it isn't). No matter what comes out on the page, keep writing for 10 minutes. Go.

What is today's date?

Now, do some math: Think of today's date in the year your mother was five. In your mind's eye, think of where she lived on that day. What city? Maybe you've seen photos of the house she lived in. Maybe you've visited it. Maybe you're just going to make up something that might have been where she lived when she was five. Imagine her kitchen.

It's this day of the year when your mother is five and she's sitting in her kitchen having breakfast. Can you see the table? What is she eating? What is she wearing? Who else is in the room?

On this day in the year your mother is five, who else is living in her house? Which of your aunts and uncles, her brothers and sisters, are there? How old are they? Can you see them? Has anyone in her family not been born yet? Is her grandma or grandpa there? Anyone else? Is her dad at home? If he isn't, where is he?

Now, imagine her mother, your grandmother, standing by the counter. What's she doing? What's she wearing? How old is she? When your mother is five, how old is your grandmother? What do you see as the feelings between your mother and her mother?

Now, on this day in the year your mother is five, what is going on outside your house? In her neighbourhood? In her city? In the world? She may or may not have been aware of this when she was five, but you know more of her history. Did anything happening outside have an impact on her world inside the house? If so, how?

Now look again at your mother sitting at the table when she was five. This little girl doesn't know what's going to happen next, but you do. This is the story you're going to write: what happens next from her perspective. Give her a hug and tell her everything's going to be alright.

Now allow your brain and heart to come together. You're going to write for 10 minutes capturing this moment from your past. Your mother, her house, her family. Keep writing even if it's garbage (it's not). No matter what comes out on the page, keep writing for 10 minutes. Go.

THOUGHTS ON MEMORY

Memory is a strange thing. How does it even work? Where is it even stored? In the brain? In the stomach? In the heart? How can memories suddenly appear or disappear? In a workshop an elderly woman confessed after the visualization exercise that she had no memory of her life when she was five. Her mother had been sick and sent her young daughter away for a year to be cared for by another woman. "And I don't remember a thing. And what's more I've decided I don't want to find out." Another woman told us she had been in a car accident and had lost her memory. She hoped that the exercises in the workshop might awaken some glimmer of her mother who had passed away years before.

Everyone who has written their mother's story has experienced a moment when they realized there were gaps in what they thought they knew, or when they discovered that something they thought was true was false, or when after creating a sequence of events they had a whole new interpretation of the facts as they knew them. Using facts in a story does not require imagination to make them better (which would be a lie) but to imagine how they might have gone together.

In the visualization exercises some people are happier imagining their own childhood than that of their mothers, whereas others prefer "making up" what might have happened in their mother's childhood kitchen by amalgamating photos, stories, and memories and anything else that could be considered a fact of her life. Siblings will tell different stories of the same woman who bore them but had a different relationship with each of them. In all cases we do the best we can to tell a story that is true.

Here's a fun exercise: If your mother is still alive compare her vision of her kitchen when she was five to what you imagined it might have been.

MY MOTHER'S HOME

Many people come from somewhere. My mother's family are United Empire Loyalists, descendants of the British who gave up their homes to come north to Canada during the American Revolution. My grandparents lived on a farm that had been in the family since 1783. When I go there I feel a deep connection to the stories I know and my memories of the place, and yet I also feel detached and irritated; the farm was sold years ago and none of my relations live nearby anymore.

There are also many people in the world today who feel like they come from nowhere. They may know of ancestors on one side or the other who once lived in a particular country or province, but the connections to that place have been severed or diluted for centuries. The ideal in the United States for many years was for citizens to deny any personal heritage and claim to be only an American. Japan has strict rules on immigration, and so it's assumed that everyone living there is Japanese since the beginning of time. There are thousands of people in Europe who could claim kinship with a valley or province, but their ancestral nationality would depend on who was in charge of that land that year. Land reclamation projects over the centuries have meant some people describe themselves as ethnic Germans in Hungary or Protestant Irish in Ireland. For many people "Where do you come from?" is a question with many answers.

Where did your mother call "home"? It may be a place her family lived for centuries or one special place in a long series of moves where she was happy. It may be a place she never visited but where she felt a kinship. It might be a country, a town, a house, a bed. It might be a lab, a kitchen, a stage.

Maybe she loved this place; maybe she felt trapped there but connections of one kind or another held her fixed. Regardless whether your mother is still living or passed away a long time ago this exercise asks you to speculate on the place where she felt the most connected to herself, the environment, and others. It's not a common question we ask ourselves or others but the answers are always informative. If you're hesitant about an answer, try asking yourself first: Where on earth do you feel most at home?

Exercise: Home to My Mother

If you don't know for sure where your mother considered home, make it up. Decide now, from the stories she told or the stories you know of her, the one place where she might have fit in, was known, where her heart was filled.

It may be you've chosen the "correct" place. It may be your own fantasy projection. But in describing it, you have grounded your mother to a physical reality that will give you insights into her character.

Describe this place: its physical attributes, social connections and history. See your mother in this place and describe what she's doing.

How do other people describe this place? Is there a secret description you have of it that no one else knows? This could be part of your memories of this place—the smell, the sounds, an event—or something specific your mother said. Go wild—fill up a page with words and drawings, maps and photos!

When people lived, worked, worshipped and played with the same people all the time, you can see how they might want to conform to one set of rules to stay in the good favour of their peers. Today people move around, working in one world, socializing in another, connecting with friends on the internet a world away, talking to neighbours from different cultures. And each group has their set of rules with their own "tells," as they call them in poker, that signal whether someone belongs to that group or not—which fork, which dress, which attitudes are "right."

We can see this shift from living in 'one world' to living in 'many worlds' in some mother stories, as mothers try to negotiate the often-conflicting rules. It's possible to see cultural rules that trace back to Portuguese or Spanish heritage, for instance, but there are also rules of behaviour in the culture of affluence, with differences in various subsections: East Coast wealth, old money, new money, Hong Kong wealth and South Asian wealth. There are rules governing wives of cops, wives of construction workers, wives of alcoholic construction workers, and alcoholic wives of construction workers.

In *The Glass Menagerie*, the character Amanda Winfield holds to the values of her wealthy and influential family even though the money is long gone. She tries to teach her children rules of behaviour that make little sense in their impoverished world, but to her, these are the standards of civilization.

We each have feelings on what constitutes civilized behaviour, and so did our mothers.

EXERCISE: MY MOTHER'S RULES

How the rules influenced each mother can be seen by the choices she made in her life. What cultural group did your mother most strongly identify with? The neighbours? Her church? Your father's business? Her business? Family? Someone long dead?

Think of it this way: Whose opinion did she most value on whether she was behaving or dressing appropriately?

Can you remember a story or incident that demonstrates this?

EXERCISE MY MOTHER'S TABLE

Describe the rules of dining you were taught in your family. Maybe your mother taught you these rules; maybe it was someone else. Imagine you're describing them to someone in China where they don't have forks (or if you're living in China, someone in the US who doesn't have chopsticks).

Some questions to get you started:

How is the table set?

Are dishes passed around the table, set in the middle, or do people fill their plates somewhere else?

Are there napkins or ways to keep hands and clothing clean?

Does everyone sit together or are there separate groups?

Who eats first?

How is a special meal different than a regular meal?

Are there special dishes and when are they used?

Whose idea of manners did your mother copy? Her mother's? The neighbours? Martha Stewart?

Describe a meal when your mother was embarrassed.

Describe a meal when your mother was proud or happy.

Thinking about eating and manners, was there a habit or condition in your home around food that you took as normal but later found out was somewhat unique?

Here are some examples:

When we exhibited poor table manners, my mother would hiss "Thrasher!" which we knew meant we were being uncivilized. When she was a child, hired men and neighbours would come to her parent's farm every fall to bring in the harvest, and one of the jobs they had was thrashing the grain—hence the name. When these big, sweaty men sat at her mother's table for dinner, they were more concerned about eating than manners. As a child, my mother's job was to slip between two men at the table, pick up the bowl one had carelessly just set down, and place it beside his neighbour who would spoon out some food and put the bowl down in the same place. She'd then take the bowl and pass it to the next man. With one word we knew her disgust for selfish people who didn't pay attention to the needs of others.

Chris's mother never sat at the table to eat with the family. There were five kids and a small kitchen, so she hovered around the table, filling plates with food from the stove until everyone had eaten. Then, before she started the dishes, she sat at the table by herself having toast and tea. It made her uncomfortable to the point of sickness when there were special meals, like a wedding banquet, when she had to sit while people ate.

What was your mother's habit around eating?

EXERCISE: MY MOTHER AND SEX

The birth control pill became popular in the 1960s, becoming one of the first means whereby women controlled reproduction. This is still a controversial idea in many parts of the world. However, it wasn't the only means of controlling when children might happen.

Which birth control methods did your mother use?

Don't worry if you don't know the answer. Maybe she didn't tell you; maybe she thought you were too young to know; maybe smart (sophisticated/ civilized/ modern/ religious) people didn't discuss things like this; maybe she didn't use any.

If she didn't tell you, based on conversations overheard and what you know of your parents, what means might she have used?

What did she tell you about sex?

These questions aren't meant to shame you. Women have had to consider these issues for themselves since the beginning of time. Thinking about your mother having to deal with questions related to her body may give you further insights into her character; you may see how her beliefs (whether you knew them or not) influenced your own. Through this lens, you may see her more as a human being rather than just a mother.

Maybe she was devout; maybe she was agnostic; maybe it was complicated. What was your mother's relationship to the spiritual realm? How did this belief play out in her life?

> Brian's mother had trained to be a nun. She followed all the tenets of the Catholic Church but, digging beneath the rhetoric, he realized she paid lip service to it all but had a firm belief in leprechauns.

Did your mother's religious practice change over the course of her life? Hint: the times where your mother's spiritual practices changed is a good indication of changes also happening in her interior life. What was going in her life at these times that may have prompted her to reconsider her fundamental beliefs?

EXERCISE: MY MOTHER AND MONEY

Credit cards weren't common until the 1960s (and in the US, many women were denied cards in their own names until 1974). I remember seeing my first bank machine in 1978. Life before that meant standing in line at your one and only bank before 3pm to sign a piece of paper to hand to the teller to get the cash you needed for the week. I can hardly believe how hard it was, and I was there!

Life had to be simpler because there was so much organizing involved in doing anything beyond the regular course of your life. Travelling was rarely spur of the moment. You could only use cash or cheques (locally) without going to the bank for traveller's cheques or money wires. You had to plan ahead for every detail to know how much cash you would need. So much worrying was spent on keeping it safe.

What was your mother's relationship to money? Was she the one who handled it in your family or was it your father? Did she spend or save? What's a story that shows her beliefs in money?

Muhammad Yunus, the Bangladeshi banker who received the Nobel Prize in Economics for developing the practice of microloans, only gave loans to women because he said they were much more likely to use the money to provide for their families. Does that fit with your experience of your mother?

How your mother used money gives insight into her character and may give insight into your own.

An interesting question to ask throughout your mother's story is "Where is the money coming from now?" It wasn't just Karl Marx who said that all events of history are attached to money. Some people grow up intimately involved in the finances of their families, going out at a young age to be able to pay for their own clothes or hand in their wages to help feed and clothe others. Many other people grow up protected and oblivious to the concerns of their parents for how they pay for anything. Your mother may have been in either category; you may have grown up opposite to her or the same. As adults we've all had to figure out where the money is coming from, where it is going and who must be appeased to keep the flow constant. Perhaps concerns for money are the impetus behind some of your mother's decisions.

Students in the future will marvel at how women in the past lived their lives and especially by how they navigated the restrictions forced on them by their society simply because they were women.

The mother of a friend of mine was one of the first airline stewardesses in a literally fly by the seat of your pants industry of the 1930's. When WW2 started many of the men in her company went to fight. She moved inside to a desk and was taught how to determine the weight capacity and threshold of each flight. This was and is a crucial aspect of the airline industry and in her time was accomplished with equations and slide rules. When the war finished the word went out to all the women working in factories and at desks that the returning soldiers needed jobs and it was their duty to vacate their positions and let life return to "normal". My friend's mother could see the sense of this and taught her male replacement all of the calculations needed to save lives. She happily went home and had babies but it galled her to hear people then say that women didn't have the mental capacity to do this kind of job. "Why did I put up with that?" she asked while telling me her story. "I should have said something." We then realized there was no one to tell.

Is there an event, perception, or choice made in your mother's life that was solely based on what someone said a woman could or could not do? Describe it in detail so people will know the rules of her society that forced it.

WHAT MAKES HER STORY UNIQUE

Good stories are like a roller coaster taking readers from drama to drama, filled with screams of laughter and tears. However, when we talk about our mothers, many people tend to flatten out everything to make her appear to be the same as everyone else, nothing special. They do not look at or for the drama that was inherent in her life. Perhaps they do this so she won't be criticized or because they were taught to not ask questions. Perhaps they are uncomfortable with a woman like their mother being considered extraordinary and that any attention given to her (good or bad) would fill her with shame. This makes a very boring story. And it actually isn't true. The human race wouldn't exist if women's lives were that boring. You don't need to make up things to make her story better. Just look specifically at where her life was unique, where things happened that weren't "ordinary". Did you ever wonder about something in your mother's life that seemed odd? Now is your chance to explore your curiosity.

EXERCISE: MY MOTHER AND MUSIC

What was your mother's relationship to music? Did she play a musical instrument? Even if they couldn't sing or play a note, some people have lives that revolve around music. Do you have a memory of your mother and music that reveals her tastes?

If music wasn't her thing, describe her relationship with another passion—gardening, cooking, dance, poetry?

EXERCISE: MY MOTHER AND THINGS

Telling the story of "how things were" involves people and relationships but it also involves things. Your kids and future generations will not believe aspects of life we take for granted now. It could be how we use an object but also how we spend our time. A new invention is novel, then accepted, then you can't imagine life without it, and then there'll be a time when you can't remember what it's for.

Look around your room. How many objects would have existed when your mother was a girl? Anything associated with a computer is out, of course, but remember plastic only became common after World War Two. It's surprising to see there are still many objects made of wood, metal, glass and cloth fulfilling functions as tables, chairs and lights, as they've always done. How many of them will still be in use 50 years from now? Will we be living in a Star Trek world of modular plastic? Or will plastic have disappeared?

EXERCISE : MY MOTHER'S USE OF THINGS

Describe an object common in your mother's life that you now see as strange. Ceramic gods? Hair rollers? Garter belts? Cake mascara?

A line of my ancestors were blacksmiths for hundreds of years and yet within 30 years at the turn of the last century, that occupation and all of the technical knowledge associated with it were made almost obsolete by the invention of cars. People around the world wore hats for thousands of years and hat makers had an illustrious history of artistry and craftsmanship passed on from one generation to the next. By the mid-1960s, almost all that finery was gone.

Is there a way of life that was common to your mother that no longer has meaning in your life?

Exercise: My mother and talking

Did your mother talk or not?

Some mothers kept rigorous contact with family, friends, neighbours and beyond, feeling it a right, obligation and necessity to find out and report on everyone's daily business. Other mothers missed the memo that said they should know where their adult children live.

What were your mother's habits for staying in touch?

Who did your mother like to talk to? Family or business contacts? Neighbours or shopkeepers? Her family and not your father's? His family and not her own?

Is there anyone she didn't talk to?

Many writers have made statements like "My mother was the glue that kept the family together." Do you have that feeling about your mother? Do you think this was determined by how often she talked to people in your family or by something else?

Some women say that their job is to manage the emotions of others – talking people down, distracting temper tantrums, cheering someone up. Was this your mother? Was she good at it? How was she at managing her own emotions?

Regardless whether she talked or not, what was your mother's preferred way to communicate? In my childhood most people had home telephones but not in my mother's time. Some people still don't have telephones. Or they skipped over land lines and went straight to cell phones.

Did your mother have a telephone when she was a girl?

How would she arrange a meal with friends? By phone? By post? Only when she met people in person?

When she was a young woman, how far away did she live from her family?

How far away were her friends?

Did your mother write letters? Does someone still have them? Letters are a valuable resource for historians and genealogists to see relationships between people and also to confirm births, deaths, occupations and other statistics.

In many parts of the world, when people moved away during the 20th century, their family and friends said goodbye knowing there was a good chance they wouldn't see them again. Did your mother have that experience?

Shop talk is the slang, attitudes and phrases used in any business. It is the private language insiders use that is only understood by those who belong. Many people consider it rude to use shop talk when away from work as it causes the people not in that business to feel stupid and excluded. Today many people use acronyms or the initials of a company or product in their conversations causing the same distress in people who are not familiar with what they mean.

Contrary to the rules you may have learned about polite conversation, shop talk is great to use in your mother's story—if you explain what it means. In a story or script, shop talk gives authenticity to dialogue. "Pushing tin," "herbaceous borders," and "big ticket items" are the kinds of phrases bandied about offices, garages and dinner tables that people of the future will find fascinating.

When Mary describes her mother Lily Rose's accomplishments in turn-of-the-century London, she uses phrases common in the day:

> Her father was what in those days known as a job master: he owned a fleet of carriages and horses for hire, which as time went by became Daimler Hire. They did weddings and ferried debutantes to be presented at court. Lily, too, was adept with horses, riding side-saddle as was the custom for ladies at the time. She could drive a four-in-hand—a large carriage drawn by four horses—from an early age. During the Great War, Lily graduated to motor vehicles and became chauffeuse to self-made tea magnate, provisions millionaire and yachtsman Sir Thomas Lipton.

One hundred years later many of these terms had become archaic, but Mary remembered how they intrigued her when she was a child and by how proud her mother was to use them.

Write your mother's favourite words or phrases. It doesn't matter if they make sense. Write fast without thinking so more can rise to the surface of your memory.

EXERCISE: MY MOTHER'S WORLDS

"When I became a mother I never imagined the worlds I would learn about by looking over your shoulders." That's a quote from my mother, Jean. My mother has learned about police work, computer design, interior design and the entertainment industry by listening to her daughters. That's what we talk about now, but when we we re little, around her table, we learned about farming, cooking, sewing, teaching, community service and genealogy. These are aspects of life that have shaped us even though none of us has followed her or my father in their work.

Have you ever had to explain to someone outside your family the meaning of a phrase or word that was common to your family? A friend of mine recounts explaining to a friend that "hanging the blacks" in her family did not signify racist tendencies but referred to a big job that started a project. Her family were theatre folk and hanging the black curtains on the sides of the stage was one the first tasks in getting a theatre ready for a season.

What were the worlds you learned about around your mother's table? These may have referred to your father's work, your mother's work, or the interests of other family members. Shop keeping? Farming? Fishing? Opera?

EXERCISE: MY MOTHER'S PRACTISES

What were some of the practices common in your mother's life that astounded you? Maybe they drove you crazy; maybe you thought them quaint; maybe you didn't even think about them until now. It could be how she managed her hair, how she baked ham, the rules she had around meeting with her friends, what she ate for breakfast. Did she have any rituals? Around making or drinking coffee or tea? Around playing cards or other games? Did she have to clean the house before going on vacation? Did she clean the house before the cleaning lady came?

Write everything down that comes to mind without thinking too much. Nothing is too common or too exotic. If you remember it now, it's worth mentioning.

My mother loves clothes. For years she made her own as it afforded her the opportunity to really dictate what she wanted. She taught us all how to sew as she taught many high school Home Economics classes. It was years before I realized how much she loved the engineering of sewing, trying out more and more complex patterns, and how she relaxed in the full absorption that sewing required.

I was also astounded that my mother had so few clothes when she was a young woman compared to what I had in my closet. She told me she had a business jacket, two white blouses, four skirts, maybe five sweaters, three dresses and a pair of dungarees, or what we now call jeans. One time, when they were moving and everything was packed away, she made my father go out and buy her a dress so she could be "properly dressed" to go to a restaurant. Women in her world just didn't wear jeans outside the house. They always dressed up, but their closets were so small!

What clothing of your mother's do you remember? Describe a piece you loved. Where was it made? How much did it cost?

Describe a piece of your mother's clothing you hated. Why did you hate it?

Describe any jewellery she had. Where did she get it?

THE MARKET AND THE STATE

"For the first time in history more people die from eating too much than too little,
from old age than infectious disease, and more people commit suicide
than are killed by soldiers, terrorists and criminals combined."
~ Yuval Noah Harari, *Sapiens: A Brief History of Humankind*

You wouldn't know this was happening from watching the news or listening to the fears and anxieties of others. When traditions are being turned upside down and centuries old institutions are morphing or crumbling it's easy for people to assume that we have gone to hell in a hand basket. But statistics show the world is safer, healthier and more prosperous than ever before.

Harari's opinion is that this safety and prosperity have come mainly from the rising influence of the state and the market over the traditional human organizations of family and community.

Wait a minute! In My Mother's Story we look pretty closely at families and community especially as they relate to our mothers. We think they're good. And so does Harari. His statistics show that the health and happiness of individuals are much better if they are in close relationships like a family. But that's not how families and communities were used in the past. Five hundred years ago families provided all the education, food and provisions needed for their members; there was no one else. Conformity, obedience and loyalty to the head of the family or community was absolute. If you didn't follow the rules you were punished or cast out and that had real consequences.

Many of Shakespeare's characters fight against the constraints of their family or a community that does not acknowledge their individual passions, opinions and interests. When a character like Romeo was banished (or ban-i-shed as we like to say in iambic pentameter) friends and family would shun him. To them he didn't exist. There was no middle class to give him a job. There were few stores where he could buy food. To survive he would have to live off the land, stealing, fighting and most likely becoming a bandit. This was how life was for thousands of years.

How many of the rules of living we were taught growing up were based on the need to survive a life of imminent death from starvation or violence? How many of them still apply?

There is still a need for families with rules and responsibilities. For all our progress, the market without education can make people into shallow consumers and blind adherence to a state can be an Orwellian nightmare. How will the new rules we write speak to the anxiety and despair of so many today who see suicide as their only solution?

By writing your mother's story you have a glimpse of the good and the bad of these forces as they played out in your mother's life. What we retain from the past as we move forward into this brave new world should be the discussion of every society on earth.

CRONE WISDOM

As our world evolves, as women take up more and more space in the landscape of our lives, the wisdom of the grandmothers will take on more and more importance. But are we recognizing and saving the stories of older women? Many people find they want to skip the last 30 years of their mothers' lives and concentrate on the good stories when she was in her "prime." It's like, beyond travelling a bit and playing with grandchildren, we believe nothing interesting happened in our mothers' lives after we left home—that she had hit her "happily ever after." Or not. Some women had very sad endings and others never lived to see this stage of life.

How will we dream for our own crone time if we don't acknowledge what really happened in this time for our mothers? This is where the arc of her story resolves; it's where she demonstrates the values she held most sacred, either by what she did or by what she didn't do with them.

For some women post-menopause is a time of freedom from the daily demands to provide for others, whether it was as mother, daughter or sexual partner. These later years became a time to think about and care for themselves, to do what they'd always wanted to do. For some this change was so radical it meant becoming "someone else," a person of such different appetites and values that they were almost unrecognizable to friends and family. Still others found this to be a time of sorrow, when they mourned their lost identity as primary caregivers and, unable to shift, found their lives lost meaning.

Unlike men, the passages of women's lives are defined in mythology by their fertility: the virgin, the mother, the crone. To people who only value fertility, the crone means "no longer useful." She is the old woman with the hooked nose who lives by herself, dispensing potions or curses. She is the grandmother who bakes cookies and avoids conflict. She is the evil woman who tries to control the lives of everyone in her family. In the Bible, the widow (who may be young or old) has the lowest status in society. Without a husband or father to protect her she must beg and scrape for the means to support herself and raise her family (if she has one). In Hollywood, the roles for older women are sometimes referred to as "witches and bitches." These icons continue to define how we expect older women to behave.

These are, however, not the only options. From a physiological point of view, humans, along with Orca and pilot whales, are the only animals that experience menopause. In all other species, females continue to reproduce until they die, or looked at another way, die shortly after they stop reproducing. What are women supposed to be doing with all this extra time? Once medical science reduced the incidence of mothers and children dying in childbirth (which was so common, women in the Renaissance were encouraged to write their wills when they discovered they were pregnant), the life expectancy of women has been much longer than that of men. So there have been centuries of old ladies doing something in their later years that's very important for the human race. But, given that they're also prone to being considered invisible or irrelevant, there are few records on what that was.

Resident pods of Orca whales are led by post-menopausal grandmothers who it turns out know better than most where the salmon are hiding. Granny, or J2, was the leader of J pod, which lives just off Vancouver Island. She was estimated to be over 100 years old when she died recently.

Speculation on why menopause evolved in whales and not in other species like elephants, who are also matriarchal, has led to the idea that older females stop reproducing so as to not compete with their daughters. (I can hear many women scoffing at this idea.) The future of the pod is better assured when the leader is mindful of the health of the whole group and not just her children.

Of course, we're not supposed to transfer the attributes of one species to another, but when there are just three species going through menopause, you have to ask what made older female humans so important they needed to stick around? What wisdom do older women possess that's equivalent to salmon hunting? In the 16th century, the Iroquois Confederacy in eastern North America influenced European settlers on many of what later came to be considered American ideals. Sadly, one idea that didn't catch on was the Council of Grandmothers. Like the whale pods, tribes were led by grandmothers who regularly met to dispense justice, decide marriages and look out for the whole nation. The council would decide on who, usually a man, would be their war chief, the person who met and spoke to the settlers and other first immigrants.

There are a growing number of women today who declare the time of the crone to be the time of freedom. The baby boomers have entered this phase of life, and many women are not stepping back, stepping down or becoming invisible. It remains to be seen what they will do with their time.

When you go out into the woods and you look at trees, you see all these different trees. And some of them are bent, and some of them are straight, and some of them are evergreens, and some of them are whatever. And you look at the tree and you allow it. You appreciate it. You see why it is the way it is. You sort of understand that it didn't get enough light, and so it turned that way. And you don't get all emotional about it. You just allow it. You appreciate the tree. The minute you get near humans, you lose all that. And you are constantly saying "You're too this, or I'm too this." That judging mind comes in. And so I practice turning people into trees. Which means appreciating them just the way they are.

Ram Dass

Part IV

WRESTLING
WITH THE ANGEL

THE POEM GETS WRITTEN. I HAVE WRESTLED WITH THE ANGEL AND I AM STAINED WITH LIGHT AND I HAVE NO SHAME. THE MOST REGRETFUL PEOPLE ON EARTH ARE THOSE WHO FELT THE CALL TO CREATIVE WORK, WHO FELT THEIR OWN CREATIVE POWER RESTIVE AND UPRISING, AND GAVE TO IT NEITHER POWER NOR TIME.
—MARY OLIVER, THE ARTIST'S TASK

If you have ever suffered writer's block you know how formidable that wall of resistance and insecurity can be. Pounding on it only makes it stronger. Take heart. Some people have found that after finishing the simple story of their mother, a story with no money, fame, agenda, or purpose attached, their hearts were so engaged and they received such positive feedback that a sneaky back door opened in the wall of their resistance. They were able to look at other projects with ease and flow—like a cork had been taken from a cask. Finish your story and you will feel like an amateur gardener planting

79

zucchini—it works! I can do it! This chapter will help you work through any blocks you have writing your mother's story.

Through this project I've discovered I'm not the only one with years of experience dealing with procrastination. Go figure! Not working is often one of my favourite occupations. There will always be an excuse to not sit down. I know one woman who, rather than write about her mother, did two years of income tax instead. As a child I played a game of pretending to write with a desk and pens and paper, and sometimes, sitting at a desk as an adult with nothing happening, I am reminded of that.

What is the difference between musing and fear? Fear will make someone else's casual desire into my highest priority. Fear puts up obstructions to getting to my desk and dangles very important emails that must be answered beside clever Facebook posts. Musing? Waiting for the muse often doesn't look like anything at all. Writing about ones mother means excavating layers of life where all the dirt and dust to be sifted is internal. In the mode of musing, staring out the window could be considered writing. Walking around the kitchen or around the block is writing. Taking a bath is writing. For some people writing is moving all the downstairs furniture upstairs and all the upstairs furniture downstairs. If you're listening within, you're writing.

Some people have found that they need to have order in their outside life before they can free this inside discussion. If that means you need to leave your partner and get settled in a new place before you can write, so be it. This is one of the reasons this exercise shouldn't be compulsory: Every person has their own process that takes its own time.

And know that when the muse arrives the words will come out very fast and the story will be completed in minutes. Be ready to fly with her when she calls.

RESISTANCE

Remember that the story you write now will not be the definitive story of your mother. All you can write is the perspective you have now. A few years from now, or maybe when you want to tell your mother's story to a new person, you will find your choices of anecdotes and descriptors might shift. Maybe you'll find some new information, or a resentment or guilt around her might finally disperse. You'll find a new story forming itself in your mind. For now, though, all you can do is write from where you are.

In his book *The War of Art*, Steven Pressfield says that the more we need to undertake a creative project the more resistance we will face. He objectifies "Resistance" as the blocks that come up when we make moves for change, for freedom, for better health. Our ego wants everything to stay the same and will try any number of dirty tricks to get its way. Pushing through is the only course of action against it.

Often resistance takes the form of huge emotions—grief, anger, frustration, shame. When dealing with profound emotions, it's sometimes useful to sneak up on your story sideways to temporarily diminish the importance of your product. Say to yourself (or to the room) that you're just fooling around with an idea. You're not really writing, not really talking about your mother—you're just experimenting. You don't really know if it will even work, so it's not worth stressing about. Then write a little bit, a little bit, another bit until you've got something on the page. Take as many breaks as you need but keep coming back.

The work you've done is a way of using your left brain, gathering dates and names and facts to avoid the emotional morass of the right brain. Some people are surprised by what they've written; others find nothing new. Nonetheless, those dates on the timeline will keep you focused and moving forward when you start to integrate emotions. Dates become fence posts and a way of breaking up the enormity of a project so writing between one post and the next is sometimes all that's needed in a day.

People come at their stories in different ways and with different needs, always looking for the release that allows them to write.

- Lisa was so enmeshed with her mother and the emotional burden of her mother's schizophrenia that she had to write in third person ("There once was a woman named Bodil") as if speaking of a stranger.

- To find emotional detachment, Jean wrote her mother's story in point form, itemizing tragic details and moments of joy, one by one.

- Some people have found release in writing as if their mother were speaking in her voice, telling her own story.

- Jennifer wrote her story as a letter to her mother, who had passed away, to tell her about the joy and wonder of the grandchild she had never met.

WHEN YOU'RE STUCK

Yes, not if—but when. We all have points in our stories where we stop, unsure how to go on. As in life, there are times when the road gets rough and we think there's no map.

Don't give up! This book is the map! And know that your story will be a map for someone else who needs to read how your mother coped with the strange, brutal, awkward, complex, mystifying moments of her life. When you figure out how to talk about these moments, they will never block you again. Remember: we're using art to do this, not therapy.

This chapter will give you some clues on how to break apart and write about The Scary Stuff. It will also give you practice in getting yourself out of the way of a good story. They are related: when broken down, much of the emotional baggage around Scary Stuff concerns our perception of what happened, the shame and guilt we, or someone else, still holds around an event. Finding the clarity to write without this cloud of emotion allows the real story to be seen.

Some people fear this project is an exercise to "out" Mom. Or blame Mom. Or victimize her. To avoid their fears, they paint rosy pictures of their mothers so no one could find fault with them or her. These stories satisfy no one. They are the platitudes, testimonials and generic accounts of women we have had to live with for centuries.

This project is about figuring out what happened, without being vindictive, and seeking to look at and tell the facts of one life without judgement. John Bradshaw, the author of *Healing the Shame That Binds You*, says parents teach their children what to see and what not to see. This is an exercise in remembering what you saw.

Fitting a life into 2,000 words means you can't say everything. But, by the same token, there's no point omitting crucial information or suspicions because they don't fit with your idea of the "perfect" life.

Some lives have just too much adventure. It's humbling to consider, once you start hearing life stories, how many people have had to navigate sorrowful, tragic, violent and incomprehensible events in their lives. However this is the story they lived through, and we honour them and their survival skills by reporting how they coped. And this kind of drama makes great stories!

Regardless of whether the scary stuff is your mom's, yours or someone else's, this is your story and you don't need to show it to anyone until you're ready.

DEALING WITH SCARY STUFF

Step One: Lock the door, close the curtains, turn the music up loud so no one can hear you. Write down the facts of your scary moments as you remember them—just the facts. Maybe write like they're a movie – image, image, image. Don't think. Write fast; it's easier.

Step Two: Look at what you've written. These facts are now outside of you and on a page. Take your time. Now you can decide what to do next.

Maybe you don't have to lock the door but know that when looking at scary stuff you want to feel safe. Do what you need to do. The threats to your wellbeing may seem huge for acknowledging there's anything less than perfect in your mother's life but the writing is actually quite easy.

What you write may not even need to show up in your final story. Here is a guideline on whether scary stuff should be included in your story or not:

- If something is a factor that changes the course of your mother's life, or influences how she made choices, it should be included.

- If something is interesting but omitting it doesn't make a difference to your mother's next step, it does not need to be included.

Therefore, if mom is an alcoholic, this likely had an influence on her decision making and should be included. If mom had an affair with her boss and only you and your sister know, this probably doesn't need to be included.

Make sense?

ADDICTIONS AND MENTAL ILLNESS

We can be addicted to so many things: drugs (legal and illegal), alcohol, cigarettes and sugar, but also gambling, sex, overspending, overworking, overeating, cleaning and exercise. And there are addictions to negative emotions like misery, fear, disappointment and victimization. These are all interesting things to consider for your story. Sometimes addictions are necessary to include, sometimes they're just a personality flavour and sometimes they don't need to be mentioned at all. As well as mom's addictions, there are the addictions of others she had to deal with.

If any addiction caused mom to make different choices for her life, it's worthy of inclusion. Addictions in others may have caused her stress but what action did she take in reaction to them? Son Billy may have been addicted to drugs, alcohol and violence but maybe all the mention needed of his part in Mom's life is to say he was "a handful." Unless, of course, Mom took out a mortgage to bail him out of jail, which he then jumped on and left everyone destitute.

In considering Mom's addictions, see if you can make a distinction between her and her compulsion. Some of what she said or did may have been part of her addiction or a side effect of the medication or cure she chose to battle it. Can you see the woman beneath this struggle? Making a distinction between her and her drug of choice will often make it easier to tell the facts of her life without judgment.

The same can be said if Mom had to deal with a mental illness in herself or others. See if you can see the person and not just the behaviour. Was she aware of her actions? Beware of diagnosing your mother. Even speculating on the page can be dangerous because it's too easy to hide behind the language of labels and use them to detach from who she was and what she did. Just tell the facts of what happened. There are ways of describing her behaviour so her symptoms are clear without needing a label. Obsessive, mercurial, impulsive—there are words that get many points across. Look in a thesaurus and get creative. It often takes just a word to encapsulate a whole disorder.

If, however, your mother was formally diagnosed with something, it's worth having that moment as a point in your story because that's a fact (right or wrong) she had to live with. Stick to the facts of what she did and said and people will see your mother in all her glory.

An interesting point to consider: could any of the people in your story have been diagnosed with post-traumatic stress disorder? At the beginning of the 20th century, soldiers were labelled as shell-shocked or as having battle fatigue. When the diagnosis was expanded to PTSD in the 1970's, the symptoms were no longer associated just with war and just with men. Any huge stress could result in a person feeling stuck in a constant sense of danger; prone to flashbacks, depression or irritability and angry outbursts. The 20th century saw its share of violence and many of the people who experienced or witnessed it were never the same again. If you suspect this might have been a contributing factor to a volatile home life, there's no need to label it. Record the facts of the behaviour but also see if you can pinpoint and include the events that may have started this condition—a car accident, sexual assault, sudden death or neglect of a child. The reader will put the facts together.

DEATHS

Death of mother. Death of father. Death of husband. Death of siblings. Death of children. Cancer, heart attack, murder, suicide, car accidents, weird accidents. There are many ways humans have found to slip this mortal coil. Regardless of the way it's left to the survivors to deal with or try to make sense of the death of a loved one. Some people have stories filled with death—10 friends dying in eight months; both parents in one day; whole families wiped out—while others seem to dodge the death of their near and dear for great swaths of time. What's normal? Both. Neither. There is no template of living against which we can judge ourselves or others to see if we're right.

Have you ever experienced a disaster and had people ask, "What are you going to do now?" as if you have a contingency plan in your back pocket for, say, asteroids hitting the Earth? There are points in every life when plans go awry and there's nothing people can do except reassess and restart. "First marks ladies and gentlemen!" they say on movie sets when they need to film another take and we all move back to where we started, back to the moment before disaster struck. In life, we can't go back in time, but we can look again at our beliefs and values to see if they hold up, to see what we need for the next phase of our lives. We can also stay stuck in despair and grief, unable to make the curve in the road life has given us.

Did your mother ever experience a profound loss? What did she do immediately after? How might this loss have affected the events and choices she made later?

I'm going to sound too gleeful here, but disasters, death and dying are horrible events to live through yet so wonderful for stories! When deciding their next step, people don't know what will happen, but you do. We know what comes from the choices they made. Tell the facts simply. Resist the temptation to skirt the emotions involved or skip over any decision making.

When I was writing the draft of my mother's story that appears in our first book, I stopped when I reached the point where my mother's anger diminished and she seemed to be at peace with the world. This was the magic moment I wanted for the end of my story: mom laughing at the table in my sister Maryann's dining room as she handed a plate of food to my new boyfriend, my soon-to-be husband, Greg. But my mother's life continued after that point and continues to this day. How could that be the end of her story? I knew I didn't need to put in my changing relationship (this was her story not mine), but I realized I might need to mention my younger sister Maryann's death a few years after that day. The grief in our family was still raw; we didn't know how to talk about it, and I questioned whether this was too private an event to include. Finally, I decided to take my own advice and just write about it first, to see if I could find words to describe the facts of this sudden event and figure out what my mother may have gone through. Just as I've written above, I had to hide away, almost locking the doors and windows before finding the courage to write.

Did this event change my mother's life? Absolutely; even though my sister was 42, we all lost the baby that day. But how did my mother change? In thinking about it, just allowing this event to roll around in my mind, I saw that my mother's life had changed because she stayed with her newfound strength and didn't collapse. Rather than denying or diminishing the magic moment I had originally envisioned for my story, this sad event became a confirmation of my mother's new strength. And that's how I framed it.

Here's what I mean by "framing an event." It does not mean writing analysis or opinions (as I've written above). It does not mean going into therapy or reliving the moments. This is where you can use art without doing harm to yourself.

At the beginning of the 20th century, Russian filmmaker Sergei Eisenstein discovered that people interpreted different stories depending on the order of film frames he edited together. He took a still frame of a woman and edited it beside a frame of a train approaching, then a frame of the woman again, then a frame of a baby carriage. People saw this and said the woman was startled, afraid that the train would kill her baby. They made a relationship between the images they were shown. Depending which images Sergei edited in beside the woman, viewers said she was angry, happy or tired—and yet exactly the same image of the woman was used over and over. The story was "reframed" by which facts were included and which were omitted.

In a workshop, Charlie said he was stuck. "What's happening with your mother at the point you're stuck?" I asked. "I'm five years old, my mother has just come home, and I tell her that dad has killed himself." Okay. (You never know what stories are waiting to be told.) After expressing my condolences, we got to work. Rather than ask what anyone's opinions, feelings or analysis might have been or how he viewed this event now, I suggested he treat the moment as a film. "Write what happened as images, frame by frame, so we see the event unfold. Do this until you're on firm ground again." He did and, in doing so, gently acknowledged a painful moment without poking at the bruises in his heart or subjecting us, his readers, to intellectual analysis.

Using a clean montage of images like this, you can also make a statement about events without using words like unfair, horrendous and tragic to describe them. As well-meaning as you may feel, these words end up being judgements on the action.

So now the big one: how to deal with writing of the death of your own mother. For some people this is the first time they've tried to put it all down on the page. If that's the case for you—do that; write everything far and wide until you're exhausted. Then take some time before you look at what you've written and ask: does this description serve the story and my mother or is this my pain? Sometimes the details are not necessary.

ADOPTIONS

I love adoption stories! So much drama! Whether a mother was adopted or adopts children or had her children adopted, these stories are filled with people struggling with what it means to be family and what it means to be human. If you are telling an adoption story, be sure to include the details of how mother and child are reunited later in life (if it happened). One woman divided her story, so her birth mother had 1,000 words and her adopted mother had 1,000 words. Other people have written a whole story for each mother.

WHEN YOU'RE PART OF THE STORY

The ideal of this assignment is that you are just a footnote in your mother's story. It takes a real shift in thinking to get yourself out of the way of a good story. However, some people play a much larger role in their mother's life than just a mention. There's a writing prompt that asks: You know what she was to you but what were you to her?

It's sobering for many of us to realize that we held a much smaller place in our mother's life than she held in ours. And that's okay! Once you get the hang of seeing life through her eyes, you'll have an idea of some of the extraordinary challenges she faced, and it's a cruel insight to realize one of them might have been you.

Maybe there was an ongoing personality clash, or there's something special about you or something special that you've done that had a direct impact on the course of your mother's character arc. This could have started at the beginning of your life (you weren't planned, you were born with a disability or condition, you were an only child), or evolved as you grew (you have an extraordinary talent, you attracted trouble). It might have impacted your mother later in her life (you became famous, you partnered with her on a venture or you had a falling out because she was religious and you were wild, or she was wild and you were religious, or she was crazy and you weren't or you were crazy and she wasn't).

Whatever it was, it can be handled simply, without a lot of words, but it needs to be included. Ongoing conditions can often be covered in a line: "I was born with cerebral palsy". If you were responsible for an event that changed the course of your mother's life write it in full: "When I received a microloan from Muhammad Yunus, the Bangladeshi banker who later received the Nobel Prize in Economics for offering loans to women, I was able to finally get my mother into a house." If you became the focus of her life for a time, this can usually be told in a sentence: "My mother always bailed me out of jail and sat in on my court sessions". The reader doesn't need to know more. We get it.

I'm happy being one of four daughters in my mother's life, but I realize in the next rewrite of my mother's story I will have to include myself a lot more to account for how this project of mine has affected her.

If you or a sibling were born with a particular physical or mental condition or your family was involved in a tragedy, you might want to check out Andrew Solomon's book *Far from the Tree: Parents, Children and the Search for Identity*. Based on many interviews and case studies, the book tells the stories of parents who not only learn to deal with their exceptional children but also find profound meaning in doing so. We are all part of each other's stories.

OTHER PEOPLE

Glynis had written her mother's story in great detail but balked at including a negative description of her grandmother, whose critical nature was a thorn in her mother's side. Glynis loved her grandmother and was uncomfortable including a negative word lest it upset her. The woman had been dead for over 50 years, so it was actually her grandmother's ghost she feared most. This is the power of family stories.

It's possible to include a fight in a story without rancour. People fight, they disagree; they have conflicting personalities. Remember this is Mom's story so if her life was changed by the ongoing feud with her sister this can be stated as a fact without taking sides. Sometimes you can identify the basic struggle of a relationship: "Mom and dad both wanted to be king." Sometimes all you need to say is, "They fought."

Not too many years ago violence was considered common in many households. Many men felt it was expected of them to beat their wives and children—for their own good, for the good of the family and/ or the good of society. And many women took out their anger and frustration on whomever was handy. Regardless whether it was a swat on the head, ritualized whippings or worse, if there was violence in your mother's home it will have a greater impact in your writing if it's presented simply —just the facts. If violence created an event that changed the course of your mother's life, it should be included but otherwise violence might just be context for how she grew up.

Many people have a hard time implicating or not implicating their fathers in the bruising that appeared on their mother's face. If she protected him, shouldn't they? There's no firm rule on this. Ask yourself if now is the time to talk about this. How much time has passed? Are any of the characters still alive? Did you witness violence or only see the after effects?

All you can do is sit with the facts in your heart and see what's important for you to say right now.

Julia asked how to write about her parents fighting all the time. I said, "Try: My parents fought all the time." "No," she said. "They really fought." I asked if there was a specific incident she could describe: bones or doors broken, someone going to jail? "No," she said. "Then," I suggested, "write: My parents really fought all the time." The anguish Julia felt was her issue with her parents, not theirs. In the 2,000 words of her mother's life, these fights were but a line.

Shirley cried and cried as she wrote of her mother being abused by her drunken father. She didn't feel able to read her story to the group. But later, she read it aloud to a friend. And cried and cried while she read. Her friend listened to the whole story and then said: "It's a sad story, but you haven't written your mother as sad. You've written her laughing and loving and finding joy in small places." Shirley realized the grief was hers for being unable to rescue her mother. In telling her story, she could finally see how her mother had made her own choices in deciding to stay with her husband.

SHAME

"I'm not ashamed of my mother!"

My, my, my! Shame is such a touchy, toxic, noxious subject. People get so defensive when you just mention the word shame—it's like they're being attacked. Or they get small and silent and you can almost see them curling into the fetal position. And I'm not saying you're ashamed of your mother! I'm saying that we have to take it as a given that any topic dealing with family is loaded with shame.

There are many different kinds of shame and everyone seems to have their favourite definition— one they assume everyone else is also using. Other languages have precise words for all the different meanings shame has in English—dishonour, insult, diminish, embarrass—but in English there's just this one catch all word. We can shame others; we can feel our own shame; we often take on the shame of someone else even if it has nothing to do with us; we can reject shame, refuse to be affected by something that someone else thinks should shame us: "Have you no shame?" Here's another distinction to try out: Shame is what you feel in relation to another person; guilt is what you feel on your own.

Shame is a big feeling, a horrible feeling. Brené Brown, author of *Daring Greatly* and famous for her TED Talks on shame, defines it as:

> ...the intensely painful feeling or experience of believing we are flawed and therefore unworthy
> of acceptance and belonging. Women often experience shame when they are entangled in a
> web of layered, conflicting and competing social-community expectations. Shame leaves women
> feeling trapped, powerless and isolated.

Try this: if you feel elastic bands suddenly clamping your jaws shut, that's most likely shame. If you feel your arms hanging like dead weights when your brain is saying Do Something, that's shame. It's that choking, red faced, tearful reaction we have to a word or thought or look. It defies logic and reason and returns inexplicably when we were sure we had dealt with it forever.

If you feel silenced when thinking about telling your mother's story, a good question to ask is: whose shame am I holding and when did it happen? It might not be your own. As children we take on the feelings that happen around our homes and it's often hard to clarify who's feeling what and if these feelings still need to be there.

Here's an example: if grandpa lost the family fortune in the stock market, for whatever reason, this is a fact. He probably felt shame—the shame of not providing for his family, perhaps of behaving dishonourably, of not respecting his ancestors who gave him so much (see how many loaded words there are in shame?). That shame is his. In the way that families are often made to take on the sins of the father maybe Mom felt embarrassed and humiliated at the time. Maybe the family's sudden poverty affected her. That was her shame then. Today these are both just facts. Does that shame, that emotion Mom felt when she was a girl mean her story can't be told?

Caroline's mother was taken from school early and as a result never felt confident about her ability to read. When Caroline wrote this in her mother's story, her mother was dismayed. They talked about it. Caroline explained that she'd written a story that told what her mother was able to accomplish in her life in spite of the fact she didn't read. There was no shame in that. Her mother was still skittish but allowed her story to be told. This is the power a witness can bring to a life.

Writing in spite of your feelings is what Brené Brown calls "building shame resistance". She charts the path from shame to authenticity: It takes courage to confront shame, which leads to vulnerability, and thus to creativity, which ultimately reveals the authentic self. That's what you're doing when you write your mother's story. The story you are writing can help you and your family transform shame into resilience.

Some dysfunctional families—and let's face it, all of our families are dysfunctional one way or another; it's what makes us interesting – use the power of words like secret and shame to hide abuse or illegal activities. It's often noted that the worse the offence, the stronger the loyalty of silence there is amongst family members. If your story is in this category, well, congratulations on considering this exercise as a way to tell your truth.

There's an adage in 12-step recovery programs: "Your sickness is in your secrets". Some people have declared that they don't want to carry the burden of family or personal shame anymore and don't want their children to carry it either. Detaching from shame filled events is the key to exposing them. This can be carried out in a series of steps.

- Assume the role of artist rather than victim, perpetrator, or whatever role your family has given you.

- Break your mother's story down into her different ages. Which age holds the greatest concentration of feeling?

- Regardless whether you know the circumstances that caused this feeling or not, as an artist you can pose a hypothetical question: if one wanted to say something about this feeling I now call shame how might one say it? Write about this. As an artist what you write will be fiction, it will be sneaking up on a feeling and a story without committing your heart or brain. When you reveal something true, you'll know it.

- It may be the shame is not hers. If necessary apply the guidelines: whose shame is it and when did it happen?

Then see how simply you can express the facts of an event. Remember: no one else needs to see what you're doing. This investigation is for you alone until you're ready to do more. However, if the feelings you unearth are too huge, consider getting the help of a therapist or counsellor to walk and talk you through the rough parts.

This doesn't disqualify you from your writing your mother's story! Think about it: once the dust has settled, these dramatic details will make for a very exciting story people will love to hear. This is not an exercise to "out" people or to be vindictive; it's to tell the facts of your mother's life through the events she witnessed and the choices she made. First write it for yourself, so you're clear on your mother's life. Then, if you wish, you'll know how to talk about it if the topic arises with your kids. After that, well it's up to you.

TOO GOOD FOR WORDS

"My mother is the best mother and I don't tell her often enough how much I love her. She had a hard life but she survived and she is always kind." Rejected mother's story submission.

Sometimes people think this project is about full, emotional descriptors of how amazing and wonderful each mother is or was and how much the writer loves her. While this may be true, it is not useful for the story you wish to tell. Regardless of the adjectives used, testimonials are generic and don't say anything about the woman being described. They are a judgement. They are about the writer—her love, her guilt, her fear—and not about the person being described. While it's good to acknowledge the sacrifices someone made for your welfare, it's more flattering if you can also recount some of the particulars of her life. Be careful with praise: is it about her or about you?

Olive knew her mother was the "best mother ever" and her story had accounts and anecdotes that demonstrated this in many ways. Her mother loved people in an easy way that Olive knew she would never be able to replicate or best. That's when Olive realized she'd always felt like a failure as a mother beside her own loving mom. It was only when she acknowledged some of her mother's limitations that Olive could see her as a whole person with a talent for mothering in the same way as Olive had a talent for acting.

A woman is not a failure if she doesn't have a talent for mothering. But mothering is a skill that everyone (men and women) can practice.

SHE WAS A MODEST WOMAN

Many of the world's religions advance the ideal of modesty for both men and women. It is a word with many meanings: not vain, not greedy, not flashy. It promotes the middle path between promoting yourself and putting yourself down, between expensive and cheap, between too much and too little. Its meaning today is used more about clothing that conceals but it is also the truth behind the phrase "Live simply so others can simply live".

Reverence, respectability, humility. The virtue of modesty has shaped the lives of women for centuries training them in what's deemed to be their appropriate responsibilities and expectations. This is the value behind the "good girl" many of us were trained to be, or, as a friend of mine described it, "being raised for othering." If you look at a gang of six year girls you can see modesty is taught and is not necessarily a natural attribute for females.

Modesty has enabled women to get along, children to be raised, and provided stability for families and communities. But at what cost? Has it been pushed too far in some circumstances? So as to not be considered vain many women have lost their voice, have lost their names, have lost their stories. In 2011 the United Nations in Egypt held a campaign for men to speak the name of their mother out loud—just her name. Many found this impossible. The evolution of modesty there had come to mean that women were often referred to as "the mother of her eldest son".

Telling the stories of women does not bring shame on them, it does not destroy their modesty. If they were to talk about themselves, that would be vain; allowing someone else to talk about them is to tell the truth of a life, regardless what circumstances are described.

In 1854, Coventry Patmore published a narrative poem called "The Angel in the House". It became wildly popular during the late 19th century and well into the twentieth as a reference to women who embodied the Victorian feminine ideal: a wife and mother who was selflessly devoted to her children and submissive to her husband.

The Angel in the House is not a person. Neither is the Good Girl. These are female icons revered by some, despised by others but without distinction. Women are human beings; they're cranky. "When momma's not happy nobody's happy." Women are crazy. They have hopes and dreams. They have voices. They have stories.

The Box on the Shelf

Usually sometime in our 20s we put all our memories, feelings, beliefs, and questions about Mom into a box and label it with one word: "Sweetheart", "Angry", "Distant", "Absent" "Drunk". Then we put this box on a high shelf with the intent to never think about it again except on anniversaries of one kind or another. Writing the story of your mother's life means finding the courage to take that box down and as an adult sort through those memories again, all the flotsam and jetsam, the hopes and dreams that were stored there by your younger self. This step of individuation allows you to throw out the lies and assumptions you made as a child and find understanding, context and connections with who your mother was. Writing her story is repacking that box in a way that it is no longer secret or feared. It doesn't really matter if your mother is still alive or passed on or even how long ago it was that she left, the process and emotions are the same. It can be painful at times when feelings associated with certain memories are replayed but it's also like housekeeping, letting old trapped air out of a sarcophagus.

Part IV and a half

GETTING OUT
OF THE WAY

This is important. So it gets its own chapter. Almost. Part 4 and a half. If you're feeling you're taking up too much of your mother's story, or worried that you might hog the limelight meant for her, here are some exercises to loosen your pen, get the words flowing and drop all expectations for the future, or shame about the past to just plunge into writing. Now is the time to get out of the way of the writing.

You will go right to the source: what bugs you about your mother. Get it out! Then maybe you'll be able to see how to tell her story without your outrage or guilt or whatever you feel getting in the way. It's not about you.

- Draw a line down the middle of a page.

- In the left column, list things you learned from what your mother did (commission). This could include things like making pastry, or a sense of justice, or how to tell a poisonous mushroom from the good ones.

- In the right column, list things you learned from what your mother didn't do (omission). This could include things like not keeping a clean house or not shaming someone. One person had "how to drive" in both columns—the good way to drive and the bad way.

- Choose one of these items and write about an incident when you remember learning this lesson, including the date, circumstances and people involved.

What I learned... from what she did	from what she didn't do

These can be long lists that you add to over time, or they can be very short. Write down the obvious answers first so your brain will continue finding answers as you go about other activities.

If you can't think of anything (it happens to all of us) think back to a moment when thoughts of your mom came unbidden into your head. "That's something my mother would do." Or, "What would my mother do now?" Chances are there's a lesson in this memory that goes back to an earlier time when you and your mom were together. That memory has influenced how you see the world. See if you can recall the first incident when this lesson happened.

Here's an example from my life: When I was a teenager we moved to a small town and my mother became a real estate agent. She needed to find new listings, which meant often driving along backroads through wild scrub and farmland. I remember her grabbing maps and saying, "C'mon, let's go and get lost!" As an adult, I realized that, unlike many of my friends, I had little fear of going off into the unknown because my mother showed me that, with maps, I could always figure out where I was, and that adventures were fun.

Now it could be that, once she realized we were on a dead-end road in a farmer's field with a growling dog, or on the edge of a barb-wired government facility facing armed guards, she only pretended that these adventures were fun, but I don't remember it that way. My mother doesn't remember saying this and neither do my sisters; my mother isn't even sure it's a compliment. However, I kept this reference in my story because it's a valuable memory for me. I didn't include the lesson; just the memory.

EXERCISE: GETTING PAST THE LABELS

This exercise can activate the issues we all have with our mothers. Yes, yes, yes, they're entirely justified, but before you get all heated up, see if you can use this exercise to challenge your assumptions about her. Answer as quickly as you can without thinking.

What is one word you often use to describe your mom to strangers?

• Describe an incident that justifies this description.

What is one word you often use to describe your mom to yourself?

• Describe an incident that justifies this description.

When you were a teen, what word did you most often use to describe your mother?

• Describe an incident that justified this description.

EXERCISE: STEREOTYPES

Would you identify your mother as a cliché? By her age, her class, her ethnicity, her culture—does she get on your nerves for being too much like people you don't like? Describe this cliché—all the mean, ridiculous and tawdry parts. Be funny, be outrageous. No one else will see what you've written. Describe their dress and appearance and attitudes about money and food. Do "her people" have expressions to describe lazy people? Or cheats? Start with "So my mother says…" and go wild, get it out of your system.

Now describe the parts of your mother that are not part of this stereotype, how she is different than these others.

If you were to describe this group of people to someone in China (or, if you're in China, to someone in America), how would it be different than what you've written above? When a cliché isn't considered common it will be seen as exotic, mysterious, beautiful. You may take the details of this life for granted but to others they will be fascinating. As a tour guide, how would you describe this aspect of your mother so she is both of this stereotype and not?

Even if you don't see your mother as a clichéd version of anything, pay attention to aspects of the culture she does embody. Exotic can be can be found anywhere and is expressed in the details. It could be the culture of miners, gangsters, Roma, deaf people, landed gentry, Jamaicans, hairdressers, French Canadians, Mennonites.

How do "those people" talk to each other when they get together? What are some of their unique beliefs? Who do they look down their noses at? Who do they admire?

The details of what you take as ordinary in your life are extraordinary to someone else.

Exercise: Me and Mom
....

Pick one or all of these prompts and write about them

- You are alone with your mother. Describe where and when, along with anything else you remember about this situation.

- You know what your mother was/is to you. What were/ are you to her?

- Did your mother have an unfinished dream? Can you see in your life an action you have taken to bridge your life to hers and complete this dream?

Exercise: My mother's luggage

Write on this topic for 10 minutes. Be expressive, unorthodox—be bold!

EXERCISE: MY MOTHER'S LUGGAGE

Write on this topic for 10 minutes. (No, not a typo!)

EXERCISE: MY MOTHER'S LUGGAGE
....

Write on this topic for 10 minutes. (No, still not a typo!)

A fact can be many things; it can allude to even more meanings. How many different ways did you think about luggage? Did you write about going on trips? Did you write about psychological blocks? Did you notice that your first thought was not necessarily the most interesting response?

Allow yourself the time and possibility to consider oblique answers. As in dreams sometimes the image of luggage stacked in the corner could actually mean abandonment, or exciting possibilities, or work done in the past. You can create your own metaphors of meaning because you have investigated your own memories and have listened for alternative answers.

EXERCISE: WRITING CONCISELY

- Pick one of the answers you wrote above and capture the essence of what you discovered in 40 words.

- Now condense this idea again into six words or less.

This is a useful exercise in which to think about editing—it's not just deleting words! Often an idea needs to be written in full first to see all its parameters before being rewritten into something concise.

SECRET OF THE CREATIVE LIFE

Here's a secret creative people know and hopefully learn to recognize so they can spare the loved ones around them the collateral damage of anguish: when you're in the middle of a creative project and it isn't working, it feels like you're dying. Literally, truly and completely dying. You cannot think of anything else, life loses its savour, and all the horrible negative thoughts you have about yourself come rushing in.

When the artistic problem is solved, it all goes away. Like it never happened!!

It makes the people around you crazy unless they recognize what's going on. This is true of musicians in the middle of compositions, writers working to deadline, artists staring at a canvas, actors in rehearsal, and people writing their mother's story. When you open your heart to the flow of inspiration, your whole being is engaged. It's a wonderful feeling. But if something you try doesn't work as planned these feelings disappear, leaving a psychic ache, a hole. It's not real.

Creative people learn: Don't take these feelings seriously; don't take them out on other people; and don't let them stop your work! The only way out is through. Keep looking for solutions; one will work, you'll be back on track, and then you'll be flooded with goodwill for all humanity.

STORYTELLING TEMPLATES

The template for many action stories comes from Joseph Campbell in his book The Hero's Journey *where he dissected the structure of many myths from around the world. Through these stories, Campbell discovered the hero (or the main character who through the process of the story becomes a hero) usually learns about self-sacrifice and duty to community.*

Here are the basics of the hero's journey:

· *Monster threatens peace of happy home;*
· *Hero reluctantly leaves home to fight monster;*
· *With the help of allies, hero defeats monster and saves home;*
· *Hero comes back to happy home changed—older, wiser; a saviour.*

Author Kim Hudson dissected movies to demonstrate what she calls the virgin's journey, the sequence of events in many character-driven stories. In her book The Virgin's Promise *she writes of many of the mythic archetypes women portray in their path to self-fulfillment. She uses the word 'virgin' in its original meaning of the person complete, autonomous, and sovereign to themselves.*

Kim outlines the virgin's journey to be:

· *Stagnant community has expectations for virgin that are contrary to her personal dreams; she becomes curious about what it would be like to be herself;*
· *Virgin finds a secret world to play and get closer to her true self, always fearing discovery;*
· *Community discovers her secret and there's backlash;*
· *Virgin wanders in the wilderness until she realizes she must pursue her dream and show her community;*
· *Someone recognizes her value and heroically makes space for her and she thrives;*
· *The community learns from her the need to love themselves as they are and the community is freed.*

The hero can be a man or woman; the virgin can be a man or woman. The hero leaves home to save it and in doing so is changed; the virgin stays home to change herself and in doing so saves her home.

When Joseph Campbell wrote The Hero's Journey *very few people undertook the hero's journey in their lives. Now more and more people are looking for ways they can "save the world." Lives following the virgin's path are less obvious but are growing more common nonetheless. These stories are of people "bucking the system," whatever that means to them.*

Maybe your mother's life unfolded in reaction to outside events like the hero's journey, or her life was more internal with choices dictated by her personal dreams. Either way she lived a great story.

Part V

PUTTING IT ALL TOGETHER

RECIPE: WRITE THE FACTS OF YOUR MOTHER'S LIFE FROM BEGINNING TO END, IN LESS THAN 2,000 WORDS, WHERE YOU ARE JUST A FOOTNOTE

Why this way?

Because separating the facts from your swirl of emotions will reveal what you know and what you don't know. Because it imposes a structure that will clarify your voice. Because you can write it fast. Because it works.

The story you write following this recipe will be your discovery draft. Some people find they like this draft well enough that it's also their final draft. Others have used this draft as a stepping off point for a longer, fuller or just different encapsulation of their mother's life.

Regardless whether you are doing this to add to the annals of women's history or to become a better writer, whether you're looking for therapeutic healing or all your friends are doing it and you want to join in, if you follow this recipe you will work through the resistance we all feel in approaching this topic and write a full story of your mother's life.

Writing any kind of memoir requires sifting through reams and reams of material. Most people quit before they start or get lost or blocked at painful events. It takes a plan to organize memories. Even the people who lost their mothers at a young age or believe they don't know enough to write anything discover they can fulfil the requirements of this recipe and tell a good story.

The silence all societies hold around women's lives is another layer of resistance on anyone who dares to sit down the write. Speed is one effective way to hurdle over these blocks to get something written. Writing is harder than editing but it has to happen first. Remember: take it one step at a time. By following this recipe, you are writing the wood before you design and build the house. You know this wood, this raw material on your mother's life. All you have to do is get it out of your head and write it down.

You will know the right time to write. Trust that. It's one of the reasons this challenge can't be compulsory for everyone in a group; some people will not be ready. But don't give up either! For some, this assignment is like a quick meal in the microwave; for others it's like a stew put on the back of the stove to cook slowly, letting the flavours meld. Maybe you need to do more research; maybe you need to read stories that other people have written in our archive; maybe you need to forgive your mother or yourself. When you're ready, follow the recipe and see what you can put together off the top of your head. This will show you the memories of your mother that are the most potent, the memories you need to look at again.

Let's break down the recipe:

Write your mother's story. It's not about you! It's not your dad's story or a letter to your dad about your mom. Or the story of your family. Or the story of your town. Those can come later. For this draft focus on following one person—your mother: what she did, where she went, what happened next. Be careful; some mothers can be wily. Even if she passed away many years ago, you might find the focus of your story has shifted off her onto a list of flowers she grew or horses she rode—anything but her.

This exercise is also about writing rather than telling. Everyone has favourite or familiar stories they could tell about their mothers, but these anecdotes rarely tell us of a person's whole life. Difficult moments are skipped, transitions are forgotten, the facts are shortened or rearranged for a gag. I am guilty of all these transgressions. This exercise requires you to look at her story again to see how your favourite bits fit in with the rest of her life. Once you've used your writing to ponder what needs to be said and how to say it, you will be able to tell this new and improved story out loud to anyone you meet.

If you have difficulty writing or have too many emotions around a particular point in your mom's life, consider telling your story to someone. They can write down the important points you cover in the interview, and then you can edit or elaborate on what they've written. This is a great exercise for friends to do together, or writing buddies, or a grandchild and grandmother. Helpful hints on how to accomplish this are included later in this chapter.

From beginning to end. This is the structure of your story. Face it: your mind is like a hoarder's house. All the memories and opinions you ever had are thrown in there together, especially the memories of your mother because she was there at so many different times of your life. The story you write here will be a chronicle of her life. Keeping a strict timeline will force you to sort your memories into the room where they belong: get the food out of the bathroom and the bed out of the living room. You may want to link thematic events together in a later draft ("she liked the bed in the living room!") or reflect more specifically on one time over another. But for this first draft, stick to "and then this happened, and then this happened." You will discover new links; you will realize what you don't know. You will thank me later, when you write your magnum opus, that you created a framework of facts here that will form the basis to any writing you do later on your mother, father or yourself. Your story will include many names and places and dates that you may know, but the only way we (your gentle readers) will be able to follow is if you put them in order. Later, you can mess everything up in creative ways, after you've found the facts for yourself.

Just the facts. Not your opinion. Not your issues. Not skirting the truth. Not what you wish had happened. Remember: there is no shame in the facts. If you have any doubts about writing something down, write it out first and then ponder what you've written. You decide what's included in your final story and how it's said. Trying to edit facts in your head to avoid saying anything about them just makes a bigger block that obscures the good stuff. It's possible and even beneficial to your story to figure out how to include facts without being graphic or judgemental. Tips on this can be found in the section Dealing With Scary Stuff (page 83).

In less than 2,000 words. You cannot fit a whole life in 2,000 words so don't worry about trying. If you were to write everything you knew about your mother you would write for a long, long time and your writing would be diluted and it would go on and on and there's a very good chance you'd get bored or discouraged before finishing.

Write everything you remember first. Then see if you want to add more facts or if you need to cut back. Making choices on what needs to be included and what can be omitted enables you to decide what story you want to tell.

Working small is a challenge but the results are worth it. Auditioning for a two-line part is harder than a lead. Large parts have lots of lines, lots of scenes; the characters have a journey that lets you warm up, flail around a bit. Small parts require you to bring everything together in one moment.

Like Picasso sketching a bull with one fluid stroke of his brush, true mastery is demonstrated in the execution of the simple.

Writer Annie Lamott has a one-inch square frame at her desk to remind her to stay focused on writing one small thing at a time.

In the 19th century, European aristocrats lived in the midst of beauty and plenty, but some realized they couldn't appreciate it properly. So, they had large—like eight-foot-square large—picture frames built that the servants set up on the lawn where they could be seen from the house. People sitting inside would see a part of their landscape framed like a painting: flowers, gardens, trees, ponds and hills. It was entertainment for the lords and ladies to find the best composition within the frame and the servants would be instructed to shift the frames back and forth until the elements within were beautifully in sync. Then, when this little section of paradise got boring, the servants would move the frames to another part of the garden. Think of a 2,000-word limit as your opportunity to focus like an aristocrat.

Where you are just a footnote. People have had different interpretations as to what this means. Decide what works best for you and your story. The intention of this rule is to keep the writer out of the action as much as possible. You can write your story in third person (there was a woman) or first person (my mother) or however it flows best from you. You are the one who chooses what stories and incidents to include, so your presence will be ingrained in the work even if you don't mention yourself. In a few cases, the writer plays a much bigger part of their mother's story than just a witness, and that is dealt with in Part 3.

Telling your mother's story means seeing your mother as a character in a movie. You don't know what's going on in her head, but you can relate the choices she made at different points in her life—these are the facts you already know. They don't need your analysis; they are what they are. But the theme of your story, what you want to tell someone about your mother, will be determined by which facts and stories you include in your story.

In therapy, you might look at how these events affect you; in this exercise, the story you write is the product, a work of art where your feelings (the artist's feelings) are not that important. It is important that you feel but not that you explain your feelings to us. You will still be present. As the tour guide, it is your story to tell—your story of the woman who played the role of your mother, revealed by the facts and anecdotes you wish to include, and by which views you consider important. Some people find it easier to write about their mothers than themselves; others feel the opposite. Whatever you prefer, writing about your mother's life will give you perspective on your own.

A SERIES OF STEPS

Remember: this draft is your discovery draft, the first step; the path to perfection is a series of steps.

Yikes! I don't want to even introduce the notion of perfection here, lest some of you think there's a perfect mother's story. There isn't. Every time you write this story, it will be a draft. Our goal is to tell the story of how we understand our mothers today. Tomorrow you might choose different anecdotes, a different theme and different facts to encapsulate her life. I have written five drafts of my mother's story already, (which my mother has rewritten twice), but I'm feeling another draft already forming itself in my mind.

The first draft, your discovery draft, is where you discover what you want to talk about. Or what you don't want to talk about. Some people decide that what they've written off the top of their heads is good enough. Great! Just allow it to be written first before you start censoring how and what you want to say.

Don't worry about how long it is. Editing comes later. The important thing in this draft is to free your voice and free your memories to capture the essence of this person.

YOUR VOICE

This draft will be in your voice because, if you've written quickly, you haven't thought of a false voice yet. Great! The most potent memories in your mind will get written first—the memories of your mother that are intimately yours, the facts that still stick in your craw whenever they happened or whenever you first heard them. If you allow these uncensored memories to be written (remember no one sees your story until you let them) you'll focus on the unique aspects of your mother, the questions you still have of her; the interesting, unmodified, politically incorrect, irrational, unresolved, awkward images of Mom. This is the material of a great story. You can rewrite, modify, edit and omit stuff later.

OTHER FAQ

It doesn't matter if you tell this story in the third person or first person: "there was a woman" or, "my mother was a woman." Some writers have realized they were emotionally enmeshed with their mothers and found writing in the third person allowed them some distance. Through this process, they were able to find the integrity of their own story. Some then chose to leave her story as that of a stranger while others experimented with saying "my mother" again.

It doesn't matter if you refer to her as Mom, Mum or by her name. Or mix up all her names. Don't worry about it. However, make sure you have her full name written somewhere in the story. After you've finished your discovery draft, see if you have changed how you reference her. It's one more interesting thing to ponder— "why did I call her Jane here?"

STICK TO THE TIMELINE

There's only one rule to keep in mind for your discovery draft: write her story from beginning to end. Don't start jumping around in time or missing bits! Chronicles of whole lives give us the opportunity to see events and perceptions but also consequences. Someone might be defeated by an event, attitude or circumstance but then find a way out, recover or adapt after some time passes. In our culture of fear, it's even more important that readers and especially children see that people can suffer trauma and survive, try something new, fail and survive. Or be devastated by a mental illness or addiction and still be loved.

Follow the thread of your mother's life as it winds through the story of her family, her home, her marriage(s) and the history of the world around her. The colour of her thread will sometimes be unique, but often it will blend with the colours around her.

It's weird to focus on one thread. Some people talk about the discipline they needed to unravel the "MomandDad" thread that is often so tightly knotted it appears to be one colour. Others comment that, after writing their mother's story, it was hard to imagine their parents even knew one another. That is a good thing!

A lot of mothers didn't like to be the centre of attention. They made sure everyone else had a cup of tea before they got their own or shooed away the camera that might not catch them in their best light. As you're writing, it may be hard to keep the spotlight on Mom. Honest. Sitting 3,000 miles away or 20 years after your mother died, you might find yourself writing about breeds of horses or Dad's necktie collection or the day the munitions plant exploded rather than letting the spotlight stay on Mom's life. Whether she liked attention or not, make sure this is a story about her. Not you; not your family. Her.

Think of it this way: in this movie, your mom is the star. So, the story of the munitions plant exploding can be told, but then the camera will swing around to see the star's reaction. If your mom didn't have an opinion or particular reaction to the munitions plant, or your hijinks on a family trip, or to your sister's frog collection, save these observations for another story. Everything here is about the star, and that's not you.

In the movie Shakespeare in Love, Shakespeare is writing what will become his play, Romeo and Juliet. When he finally hands out the finished script to his actors, there is a brief scene where the large actor playing the nurse tells a friend, "It's about a nurse." This is a joke on actors who all believe every play is really about them—but isn't that what we do in life as well? Doesn't everyone believe they're starring in the movie of their life; that everyone else is a bit player to their story? Many people only see their mother as the woman who did or didn't give them what they needed as children. They are startled to consider that she had a life of her own where she is the star and where mothering was only one aspect.

The story you write here about your mother's life is more like a movie than a novel. In a novel, the writer speaks for all the characters, telling their innermost thoughts and dreams. In a movie or play, the only information actors have about the character they'll play is what the character says, what they do and what others say about them. And sometimes characters lie. Don't put words in your mother's mouth. Allow her story to be told by what she said and did, and by what others said about her. It will be more than enough.

Get the grade one teacher out of your head. The one who says you don't know how to write. Get the university creative writing professor out of your head. The one who says, "You can't start a story with 'She was born in.' How boring!!" If you have to write, "She was born in" to get started, write that down. Or start with an image of your mom to set the stage and then head back to the beginning. Ignore all the critics in your head. Tell them, "This is something I need to do" and keep ploughing through.

The stories you grew up on, that you learned while washing dishes or walking to the store or on long car trips, are the most exciting stories ever lived. You have to believe me on this, and I've read a lot of stories. It's not about your writing style or your cleverness; it's about what happened.

Maybe you just have to get up your nerve. When you're ready, you'll know, and you really will be able to write this story in two hours. If you feel ready, let go of the branch and fly. It's safe. It's time.

WRITING YOUR DISCOVERY DRAFT

If you're feeling ready to write, here's a plan for getting your discovery draft written:

1. Pick a day two weeks from now and make a date with yourself for two hours. Write it on your calendar.

2. Forget about it. Your brain has now opened a file and will sort through everything you've remembered, recorded and wondered about your mother, without your need to intervene.

3. For your date, sit in a quiet place with a pen, computer, typewriter or recorder—whatever medium gives you strength and you can use with ease. Some people have a photograph of their mom or another reminder of her, such as a scarf, jewellry, music or scent. Some people clear away all distractions. Starting at the beginning of her life and going as fast as you can, splat down all the details of your mother's life IN CHRONOLOGICAL ORDER. Put in as many names and dates as you can. If you hit a blank patch, write down something like, "I can't remember anything here," and move on. If you have a question about what you've just said or something you don't know, write it down. Questions are often more evocative than answers. If feelings come up, let them be, and write through them. It's just housecleaning; the feelings you had when an event occurred will often surface with the memory. Just remember "It came to pass" and let the feelings pass through and out of you. DON'T STOP WRITING. Remember to write something about every phase of her life, especially after you left home and the later years of her life. Write until you reach the present day or her death.

4. Walk away from the table. Give yourself a treat—a walk outside, a bath, a good cry.

5. A few days later, pick up what you wrote and try to read it with the eyes of a stranger. Have you captured the essence of this woman? Is her life documented at least in some small way from beginning to end? Have you talked about your mom in every paragraph rather than about you, your dad, the town or the times?

6. Once you're satisfied, read it out loud to a friend. Choose the most non-judgmental friend you have. Your discussion with this friend may prompt more memories that are better suited to your story or may provide questions you didn't know needed answering. Rewrite if you want.

7. Count the words in your story. Computers do this easily; if you've written by hand, you must count by hand. 2,000 words are about three to four pages, depending on the size of the font, the line spacing, etc. This is the length of a good short story, and all stories posted in our archive must be less than 2,000 words. Forcing your story back to 2,000 words means you have to decide what's most important to say—and that will make your story stronger.

That's it. Easy peasy lemon squeezy.

BUILDING THE HOUSE OR FINDING THE STORY IN THE FACTS

Maybe you've started writing your discovery draft but feel you have a "grocery list of facts" that don't tell a story; maybe you're hesitating before writing your draft, with facts spread around and don't know how to start; maybe you've written three drafts and they're just not working; maybe you have to tell this story for a different audience and don't know how to make the shift. What to do?

First of all: Congratulations!!! You have broken through resistance and probably have most of the material needed to complete your house. Yay! By working in chronological order, you can see the outlines and tone of a story that follows the emotional journey your mother went on through her life. Yay! This is what we call the character's arc in playwriting: seeing where she started and where she ended up.

FINDING THE ARC

Some people can just write. They sit down, and words flow. Other people need a launch pad. If you can't decide what to include and what to leave out or if your story reads like a grocery list with equal weight given to all points, it may be time to let some heart guide your words, images and phrases.

Think of a moment you know needs to be in your story. It could be an image, event, sound or a realization you had about your mother. What were you thinking or feeling around that time that made this moment important? Don't worry if you can't articulate this yet. Sometimes this moment is the beginning of your story and sometimes it's the end. In Dolores' story, included in this book, she started with hats, her mother wearing hats. Nimet started with the feeling she had seeing her mother being so afraid in a new country when she'd been so fearless as a child. I knew I wanted to put the moment of my mother smiling as she handed my new boyfriend a plate of food in my story. Often, when we see the end, we can know the beginning.

If there's a moment you know needs to be in your story, look at what else you need to explain so a reader will have the same feeling as you do when they get to that point. Nimet made sure she had examples of her mother being a fearless child so there was a contrast to her being afraid later. I needed to write about my mother's anxiety so her release from it would affect readers in the same way it affected me.

Maybe you've got over the hump of getting started but, like others, feel "bored" by your list of facts. The facts of your mother's life are not boring, by any means, but maybe you need to find a theme or an image that gives you structure, to help you determine which stories you want to include in this version. Think of it this way: the facts you've written are like the boughs and baubles of a

Christmas tree that are spread out all over the floor. They look boring; they look chaotic, they are nothing like the tree you imagine. But all you need is a trunk to hold everything together in its right place.

Do you see any patterns emerging in what you've written so far? Boats or flowers or clothing or returned kindness or dreams coming true or resilience? Recurring images or states of mind? If so, they can be used as bookends or an emotional through-line.

- Sharon realized whenever her mother played the piano she lost herself (or came back to herself), from the time she learned to play as a child, through having her own children and all the adventures they had moving around the world, when dreams came true or when they crashed. So, Sharon structured her story as the movements of a classical piece of music.

Is there an image of your mother near the end of her life that stays with you—a moment that captured her essence or revealed a part of her that was, to that point of her life, unseen?

- Lana had an image of her mother in her 60s, laughing as she rocked back and forth on a swing. In that moment, Lana was startled to realize she had never seen her mother laugh before. So, when she chose which details of her mother's life to tell—the hard work and unhappiness, the war and her mother's stoic response to tragedy—it was with a mind that a reader would be as surprised and relieved as she was at this moment of joy and release near the end her mother's life.

- Barb's first memory of her mother was of her looking glamorous, putting on lipstick while looking at herself in a mirror. She finished her story with another image of her mother as an old woman, still careful with her looks, her hair coiffed back as she put on lipstick.

STORY STEW

Facts are dates, marriages, births, deaths—anything found on census records, church annals, immigration reports, military rolls. These are the bones of humanity. Stories are the connective tissue—why people moved, how they fell in love, rivalries, crimes, capers, the peculiar anecdotes each person participates in through their lifetime.

If you didn't create a timeline as described on page 48, go and do it now. The timeline will give your story structure. Chronological order means your story will start at the left end of the timeline (or a bit before) and move to the right through the events of her life. But you don't need to include everything you've written on your timeline in your story.

If your story were a stew (with apologies to vegans), there are meats, vegetables and spices.

The major events (marriage, births, moves) are the meats. These dates should be in your story. When you get lost, look back at your timeline and see what's coming up next in your mother's life. With each event you include, give a thought to whether your mother chose what happened or whether someone else chose for her.

Good stories are vegetables. Many of these dates will have stories attached: how she met your father, interesting birth stories, the war intruding on her bliss. Anecdotes like these are the bulk of your story, and you decide what you want to include to best allow someone to see and understand your mother.

Spices are her personality, which can be captured in descriptions of her clothing, the flowers she planted, the food she loved or hated, the jokes she told. How she responded to events and expressed herself are unique expressions of her personality.

Everything goes into the pot, into your story, **in the order it happened in her life.**

Remember to include stories from all the times of her life, especially after you left home. We sometimes think our mothers are doing nothing, or at least nothing interesting to us, once they're not in front of us anymore. If you're wondering about this, look at the section I've called Crone Wisdom on page 76.

EDITING

"I saw the angel in the marble and carved until I set him free," said Michelangelo.

Some say this is the most exciting step in the process; others don't want to touch their mother's story once they've finished their discovery draft. How far you go with editing depends on the reasons why you set out to write in the first place.

Regardless whether you're set for another adventure or are content with what you have already created, well done! You have gone outside the comfort zone of most of the people in the world. You have broken through your personal "mother taboo," the idea we're not allowed to speak of our mothers except in the most glowing terms, to write a story that is organized, coherent, and (you can tell when you read it to others) enthralling. Perhaps your story is 2,000 words; perhaps it's way more or way less. For your own use and pleasure, it doesn't matter! Congratulate yourself on getting the facts of your mother's life committed to paper for you and your family to remember.

Editing, however, will allow you to clarify the image you want to portray of your mother in action. You will deepen your experience as an artist, honing an artefact created from your own life and stories. You will practice writing skills you can use in other writing projects where editing is important. And you can get your word count to less than 2,000 words, qualifying your story for the My Mother's Story Archive!

For the purposes of this project, editing your mother's story can mean one of two things, which work together:

- Finding the story

• Cutting to get it under 2,000 words

Often, clarifying the story, getting specific on what needs to be said, will naturally reduce the word count. And reducing the word count will allow you to see more clearly what you want to say.

Writing the story of your mother's life required you to find a way to emotionally detach from her, to see her as a woman who happened to give birth to you. Editing requires that you stand back even further to see the whole of her life and the whole of your story of her as an entity rather than a series of events.

Artists do this all the time. They stand back and squint at their work, imagining others viewing it, trying to see their painting, poem, dance or sculpture with fresh eyes. They look for what is true and what is clumsy, awkward, ill-defined or false. There is a distinction to make here: you are not looking at what is wrong with your mother but what might be wrong with how you have portrayed her in your story.

A film is said to be written four times: first by the writer, then it's changed by who is cast in the major roles, and then it is changed again by what happens during filming, Finally the film is created again by the editor who chooses what footage will best tell a story. Film is a collaborative art and it can change considerably from the writer's vision to what appears on the screen. Many editors don't want to know what happened during filming, how one shot cost the production a big hunk of the budget; why a scene took three days to complete because the stars were fighting. It doesn't help the editor to know what a director meant to film or to know that the scene where the guns and the bananas got mixed up was a total fluke. The editor doesn't want to know the reasons or the cost; she (or he) wants to make the best story possible from the material that's presented.

TAKE A BREAK

In editing it helps to step back from you've written to be able to see it with fresh eyes. So now, before doing anything else, be an artist and put your work to the wall. Forget about it. Write something else for a while, do the laundry, look after all the tasks you've neglected while you've been working on this. For two weeks, if you can manage it. Or two days. Or 24 hours. Give yourself (and your story) the time you need to walk away from your fears and pride and shame and develop a new outlook to see what you've actually written.

Are you back now? Okay. Let's look at this story again.

As you can read in the section above on finding the story, you now have the wood and probably have a pretty good house built from it. Since your facts are in chronological order, you have already laid out the floor plan for your house. Yay! But what you've written might not be what you planned. A lot of unconscious material will have found its way onto the page. **Be ready to change your mind.** This is where editing gets fun.

Like designing different houses, you can have a different theme for each draft. One draft may want to focus on your mother's spiritual arc; another may be about recovery, another on finding herself, another on losing herself. With enough distillation and enough drafts, all of these elements can be incorporated into one story.

After facing criticism for what seemed like every point I'd ever written about her, I wrote another draft of my mother's story just for her. She read it and said, "You make me sound like such a failure!" I replied, "Well that's how you describe yourself to me." She huffed, "Well, I wouldn't want anyone to think me a Pollyanna." "No chance of that," I replied and tore it up. This draft, with a failure theme, was one I wasn't interested in sharing; it had served its purpose. My mother and I had a few interesting conversations after that, and I like to think she became more aware of the story she was telling herself about herself.

By writing down images, facts and anecdotes off the top of your head, you have not only captured a pretty good version of your true voice, but you also have found the memories most potent in your mind. These memories are the ones that have stuck with you regardless of what has happened in the intervening years; these are the memories that for one reason or another have meaning for you.

So, what have you written? Don't be too critical.

When I'm working with playwrights, there are often phrases, images or whole scenes in their first drafts that don't make any sense. Beginners are tempted to edit out all the "nonsense" to get on with the business at hand. Given the template we're using, you will still have an effective story if you do this, but you might also end up with a chronicle that seems more like a list than a movie. This happens when all the events in your story are given equal weight. You might say "That's what you asked for!" and you'd be right, but this section on editing is now asking you to go deeper.

Art is not always linear. You don't want mystery in a business prospectus, but in trying to capture the essence of a person on paper, you can get a lot more mileage with a lot fewer words when you use the model of a poem. In the work of writing your mother's story, know that if something has landed on your page, if it erupted from the endless editing that happened in your brain while thinking, "What happened next?", it's there for a reason.

Sometimes a fact needs to be distilled down to its essence to be understood; sometimes, like a jigsaw piece, it needs to be turned over and over to see where it might fit. Sometimes after long contemplation, an image resolves itself as a good idea that needs to be in another story. All this to say: Trust your instincts.

Creating something with words is often like sculpting: there is an image or sense of the whole that is being created, but it is trapped within a mound of clay or block of stone. Or it may need more clay in particular places to be whole. You have a sense of the story you want to tell, the details you consider important. With words, you sometimes delete text to reveal the true story beneath. At other times, you'll write to add and build out more in order to create the whole. The trick is to be able to hold to the essence of your story, Michelangelo's angel, that you see in your heart.

Now don't go sliding into talk of angels and hearts and mothers—save me from the card rack! In art we work, manipulate and think about details, but the whole is something we feel. Michelangelo intuited the sculpture hidden in his block of marble. He probably had a commission, probably from his Pope, so he was probably already thinking in religious terms. He looked at the structure of his stone, the flow of the grain that would determine the general shape of what could be created. And then he dreamed and saw an angel. Imagining the story in our hearts can give us access to a deeper meaning we want to convey.

You have written clues to that meaning in this story already. Since undertaking the exercises in this book—by answering questions, creating a timeline, visualizing the environment—your brain has continued to process this material. It has found a way to process the facts of your mom's life into the truth of her life, as you see it in this single moment in time.

Generally speaking, if your mother lived through many events (wars, abuse, immigration), much of her story will be taken up with descriptions of these plot moments. She will often be reacting to what is happening around her. And that will be a great story.

If your mother's outside life was relatively stable, her journey will be more internal, more character driven, and thus her story will reflect more on the choices she made to shift away from or towards a better version of herself. Another great story. For more details on this look at Storytelling Templates on page 37.

The pivotal moments of your story are those where your mother made choices, but they're often hard to recognize.

A friend took a playwriting course and wanted to write about her mother. "Don't do that," the instructor said, "you need a main character who isn't passive." Passive characters are death in dramatic form. They wait, they watch, they take orders, and serve. In drama we need to see the protagonist (hero/ lead character) make decisions, take action. There's a perception that mothers don't have minds of their own. They aren't superheroes and can only make sure other people are wearing their sweaters and are eating properly.

Was your mother passive? Really? Maybe you think your mother's life wasn't that exciting but don't confuse the so-called ideal woman, the "angel in the house" with a real person. It doesn't matter how sweet a woman is or was, there are moments when she puts her foot down, speaks her truth or goes against the rules. She slams the door. (For non-theatre-geeks, this refers to Henrik Ibsen's play A Doll's House, a modern classic and one of the first feminist plays, which premiered in Denmark in 1879. At the very end, Nora decides she will have her own life and leaves the room, her home and her husband, slamming the door.)

Even if Mom eventually went along with what Dad said, how often did she have things to say before she gave in? Or maybe she wished she could have said something, but "the rules" said she couldn't. Look at the events you've included in your story. There are moments that you, as her witness, might have thought strange, or unique or noteworthy; these may be times when your mother was making or considering a choice about something. See if you can pinpoint what might have been bothering her.

Another friend said his mother didn't have a story. "She just went along with whatever my dad said." I told him "Your mother was a transplanted Quebecois, living in Los Angeles in the 1950's selling French lingerie to movie stars. That is a great story!" Remember: the writing you do isn't about accomplishments. It isn't all about life or death moments. It's about the stories.

GETTING RID OF WORDS

So, while pondering the larger forest, let's prune some of these trees.

Maybe you have 2,000 words; maybe you have 900. Maybe you have a 12-page epic journey with descriptions of grandparents, aunts and cousins (so no one feels left out), accounts of dad's work, the contents of her garden, what happened to the store she worked in after she left. That's all well and good but remember every hoarder will tell you that every object in their home has great meaning and value. Now is the time to decide what is necessary for this story at this time.

This is a story about Mom; therefore, every fact and story bit must relate directly to Mom in some way.

Say you now have your story of mom's life from beginning to end, and you love all the bits for whatever reason, and it's 3,200 words or 2,700 words. So close and yet so far from our objective. How do you decide what to edit now?

When you're that close to your objective, there are two methods you can use to condense stories: clarifying meaning and removing superfluous words and phrases.

Writing quickly for this project hopefully got you over the "aim for perfection" hump so many people find in other writing exercises. The story here is the main thing, not how you tell it. Facts, facts, facts. Hopefully, now you see that your mom lived an interesting story. You'll see that you have written in your true voice with many of the idioms, phrases and pacing of your speaking voice. This is great! Your grade-three teacher might have wanted standardized English, but here the heartbeat of your story is the words you choose.

That said, while writing fast, a lot of people write a lot of words trying to figure out what they want to say. They'll say it one way, then another and finally a third way to clarify what they mean. These redundant phrases seem more pronounced and harder to remove if the writer isn't sure she even wants to make this particular point. There will be even more qualifiers and sub-phrases clogging up sentences. This kind of writing doesn't mean to offend; it wants only the best for everyone, it dithers on its way to the point. It is death for a story.

Now that you've written what you want to say, you can take out all the meandering it took to get there.

ADJECTIVES AND ADVERBS

In this tiny literary house you are building, every word has to justify its inclusion. Stephen King has written about his hatred for adverbs ("if you need to say, 'she shut the door firmly,' you haven't written well enough for your reader to know that of course that's how the door was shut!") but I hate adjectives. Sometimes they add a touch of colour to a description (It was a dark and stormy night), but in some people's hands they end up like exclamation points! Used at every opportunity! To make sure a point is made! Suggestion: take out every adjective and see what's lost. Put back the ones that really need to be there.

REDUNDANCY

It was a dark and stormy night. Why is this heralded as the worst writing ever? Of course, it was dark; it was night! This is a redundancy. I am quite prone to redundancies when shifting my thinking in the middle of a sentence and thus smashing two thoughts together. Look carefully at each sentence to see if you are repeating a thought.

THOUGHT PACKETS

Thought packets are redundancies that are sentences rather than just words. When I'm trying to find the exact way to say something I often write down all my choices: "It was more dark than stormy but still the rain pelted down, the dogs howled, it was miserable, I was miserable, and it was dark, very dark...." Okay, okay we get it! Look at your paragraphs again. Are you repeating yourself using different words, different phrases? Pick your favourite phrase, the winner, and cut the rest.

THAT

I am a terrible offender for this and can only think that we use 'that' a lot more in speaking than we do in writing. In this writing, which is coming from the heart and quickly, it seems that that shows up even more often. It is often unnecessary. Read your story out loud, take out every that and then put back the ones that prove they need to be there.

LISTS

More often than not, they're more about you than Mom. Try to limit any list to three items, your favourites, and cut the rest.

EDITING EXAMPLE

Rachel's discovery draft was 2,700 words long, so she needed to do more cutting but felt she had pruned everything back to what was absolutely necessary.

Before reading her story to us, she said one of the bits she wondered about was her opening, which she had written about her grandparents and great-grandparents. Rachel said, "The star of the story doesn't even show up until the end of the first page but I knew I wanted to show the family and the circumstances she was born into." Here are her opening paragraphs:

Patricia was born to Bob & Dorothy Barry on December 13, 1941, in Wetaskiwin, Alberta.

Bob's parents were originally from Ireland. When they were pregnant with their first child, my grandfather, they were set to immigrate to Canada on the Titanic in April 1912. When they arrived to board the ship, they were told that their brass bed would have to be sent separately as there was no more room for cargo. My great-grandmother refused to get on the ship without her brass bed, and they decided to book passage on a later ship. The brass bed is still a treasured family possession to this day. The family settled down in Wetaskiwin, Alberta, where my grandfather was born and grew up.

Patricia's mom, Dorothy Dunlop, was 16 years old when her family emigrated from England to Canada in 1927. There was a government incentive program that gave them the ability to own their own farm in Canada. They wanted to give their children a better future, so they said goodbye to everything they knew and moved to Canada. Dorothy loved the Canadian way of life & the freedom she had in Canada and when she was a young woman, she moved with her sister Lisa to Wetaskiwin & got a job and made many friends.

Bob and Dorothy met, fell in love and then got married. My grandfather taught my grandmother how to skate and Dorothy thought he was so modern. Theirs was a beautiful marriage that would last for over 50 years.

This is a nice description of family history, but at first glance and 253 words, it might also be considered superfluous. You can also see how important it is to not assume readers will keep track of different generations. In this case new characters were introduced by their relationship to Rachel the writer (mother, grandmother, great-grandmother). However this also emphasizes that Rachel is the star of the story not her mother.

In a first step of editing we consolidated thought packets, got rid of extra words and cleaned up images:

Patricia was born to Bob and Dorothy Barry on December 13, 1941, in Wetaskiwin Alberta.

When Bob's parents were pregnant with their first child, my grandfather, they were set to immigrate to Canada from Ireland on the Titanic in April 1912. When they arrived at the ship, they were told there was no more room for their brass bed. My great-grandmother refused to travel without it, so they booked passage on a later ship. The brass bed is still a treasured family possession. They settled in Wetaskiwin, Alberta, where my grandfather was born and grew up.

Patricia's mom, Dorothy Dunlop, was 16 years old when her family emigrated from England to Canada in 1927. Using a government incentive program they were able to own their own farm in Canada and thus give their children a better future, so they said goodbye to everything they knew and moved to Canada. Dorothy loved the freedom of Canada and soon after moved with her sister Lisa to Wetaskiwin where she got a job and made many friends, including Ken, my grandfather. He taught my grandmother how to skate and she thought he was so modern. Their marriage that would last for over 50 years.

At 198 words it's much clearer but the focus is still on generations past and not Patricia, the star.

Before cutting any more just for the sake of cutting, we looked again at what had been written, talking with Rachel about what might be behind some of her choices. How does anyone know what's right, appropriate, or wrong for a story? That's what editing is all about but it's often not obvious what falls into which category.

Rachel's story of a brass bed saving the family from death on the Titanic is something she might have heard from her mom, so maybe that was a link to our star. What other reasons might Rachel have for feeling this anecdote was important enough to keep?

- Connecting her mom with fame? (Rachel really disliked this suggestion but it might be appropriate for someone else's story)
- Evidence her mom's family is lucky?
- Evidence of her mom's family trusting their instincts?
- Explains the value of a brass bed that's still cherished?

When Rachel asks herself which reason best suits her image of the 'angel' she's creating, she will have an idea of how to edit this anecdote down to fewer words.

In the same way, her grandmother's family story is using up a lot of words for as yet unknown reasons. Could its importance be:

- To give grandma equal words to grandpa?

- To show her mom's inherited traits of gratitude and spunk?

- To show the values of grandma's English (as opposed to Irish) heritage?

- To show how grandma and grandpa got together (plot)?

Maybe one of these is correct; maybe they're all wrong, but they are all possible. Editing involves asking what you meant to say, thinking through the options and feeling which answer frees the angel from the marble.

After some consideration Rachel was able to clarify that the Titanic was included because her mother would not exist if not for her grandmother's stubbornness and insistence on not travelling without her brass bed. Patricia's strength of character was inherited from her mother who also loved adventure. Patricia's first generation Canadian English and Irish heritage were important to include so later mention of a religious conflict between Catholic and Protestant could be referenced. And our discussion pinpointed the quality of luck throughout Patricia's life.

Rachel's final first paragraph:

Patricia's life began with luck, determination and a sense of adventure. In 1912, her Irish grandparents luckily rebooked their passage to Canada because the Titanic was too crowded for them to bring their brass bed. In 1926 her English grandparents embarked on a great adventure; giving up everything they knew by moving to Canada to give their children a better future.

The grandparents are important for what they gave Patricia who is now the star of the story. 61 words.

GET FEEDBACK

When you're ready, read your story out loud to someone. This is a highly recommended step in the process, whether you want your story public or not. There's something about finding one witness to your story that finishes the process you've undertaken. It's like it seals this new way you want to see your mother and allows you to stop looking back.

Choose a person you trust to read to, not necessarily a close friend or family member. You want someone who can stay objective and has your best interests at heart. All artists collect "safe critics" who don't inflame our insecurities by passing judgement or offering advice on how they'd write (paint, compose, film, dance, sculpt) this work. A safe critic has some idea what this creation has cost you emotionally and will give you feedback on their impressions of what you've created. They are an objective mirror.

If you are doing this in a group or with a writing buddy, know that you are with people who understand how nervous you are because they are in the same boat. It's weird how, no matter how benign your story might be, you will feel very vulnerable before you read. I remember feeling very nervous (much more than in any other writing class). Don't worry about inadvertently crying when you read (or worry about not crying). Tears flow for the craziest reasons. ("A sewing machine? I'm crying about a sewing machine?") It's just another example of house-cleaning the past, of who you used to be, forgotten hopes and dreams. Your reactions will get smaller and smaller the more times you tell this story. Remember: this isn't about you.

You want to see if the person you are reading to can see your mother as a woman in the world. Pay attention to anecdotes or images you remember while reading, memories that you had forgotten—they might be useful in your rewrite. When you're finished, write down the questions your safe critic asks.

They are looking at the forest while you're still looking at trees, so their questions and comments will give insight into points you may have thought obvious, but which need more explanation. The conversation you have with your witness after reading will almost invariably unearth aspects of your mother that should be included in your story somehow. Write them down if you can so you can reference them when you next look at your text.

PRIVACY

Everyone wrestles with this issue. If there's one thing you can take away from this project, it's that human beings are not "one size fits all." Some people are concerned about Mom's privacy (even if she died long ago) and some are concerned about their own. One woman who had her mother's story told in one of our stage shows remarked on how odd it was to have her neighbours assuming they now knew who she was. It wasn't necessarily a bad thing—she had spoken the truth and was okay with all the parts of her mother's story—but she had to get used to this greater level of intimacy with people she only knew vaguely.

Our notions of privacy are changing in this changing world. I remember a conversation with a friend about the difference between living in a small town and living in a city. This is what it boiled down to: in a small town you cannot be anonymous and therefore guard your privacy; in a city, you are anonymous and therefore you can be less concerned about privacy.

We have witnessed so many stories filled with shame—unplanned pregnancies, secret adoptions, abortions, addictions, mental health issues – and the overriding impulse of each writer has been to finally tell the truth and clear the air. Through disclosure, they feel they and their mothers are finally released.

OXYTOCIN (NOT THE OPIOID OXYCOTIN)

Want to know another secret? When you finish your mother's story and read it out loud to someone, you will be flooded with oxytocin which bestows feelings of goodwill for all humanity. Oxytocin is a hormone and neurotransmitter with a lot of very interesting qualities:

- *It is released in women during childbirth and is often used to induce labour.*
- *It is released when the nipples are stimulated in breastfeeding causing a sense of well-being flooding through mother and baby promoting and perhaps creating the bond between mother and child.*
- *It is released when a woman experiences an orgasm.*
- *It is a stress remover that is released when a woman speaks her truth and feels heard.*
- *It is released in a man when he gets an "Atta boy" of praise.*
- *It is released in men in the presence of their children.*
- *Its presence in a man promotes loyalty to his partner.*
- *It's been called the Hormone of Love because it promotes trust, empathy, group identity and community building.*
- *It exists in very low levels in sociopaths.*
- *It stimulates in-group conformity and herd mentality.*
- *People given a dose of oxytocin can more easily be persuaded to lie and cheat to protect their group.*
- *It is used as a drug for people on the autism spectrum, with Irritable Bowel Syndrome, and anxiety.*
- *It supports the release of serotonin, your brain's feel good chemical.*

Part VI

THE MOVEMENT

IT BEGAN WITH A STORY.

Iwas at a wedding, waiting for the hors-d'oeuvres, listening to a friend talk, when she paused and said, "To understand what I'm saying, you have to know my mother's story."

In about five minutes, she told me all the major events of her mother's life—born here, to these parents, moved there, did this, did that. For some reason, perhaps because I'm an actor and story editor, I didn't hear this as a list of events but rather as a character arc, a technique we use in developing plays and movies. We plot out the journey of a character through the story, both physically and emotionally, somewhat akin to tracing the path of one thread through a tapestry. In fact, I saw a movie in my head of this woman's experience in England, then Vancouver, then New York; going back to England through World War Two and then back to Canada. And it was fascinating.

I thought, I wonder if I could do that?

Quickly I told my friend my mother's story, deciding in the moment what the most important events of her life might be. This was very weird. My mother did not have an adventurous life, and I had never really told any stories about her except to complain. I could feel memories popping up in all parts of my brain as I tried to link disparate thoughts together. What happened next? Finally, I made it to the end, the present moment, since my mother is still very much alive, and her story continues. I felt the movie of my mother's life wasn't nearly as exciting as my friend's, but I was satisfied that I had come up with something that approximated her journey, her arc. My friend, however, thought my mother's story was incredible. She had never heard anything so compelling. And it was so different from her own.

Throughout that evening, as speeches were made, toasts drunk, and dances danced, I thought about this exchange. How exciting it must have been for my friend's mother to have had such a life, how fate works in such different ways with each of us, how we give so little value to the familiar. I thought of the frustrations I'd had doing research for a play I was writing and finding so little on how women in history saw themselves and their lives. As an actor, well, most of the characters I auditioned for and played were clichéd: the crying mother, the stern nurse, the cheerful teacher. And there were so few of them! In Shakespeare's time and in Japanese kabuki theatre, women were forbidden on stage, so it might have made some sense that there were fewer female characters. But now? What could possibly excuse the proliferation of movies and plays today featuring five, eight, eleven men and no women? Or one pretty girl as the "prize"?

What if, I thought, women's stories aren't being told because we just aren't telling them—we, as in all of us, not just the "official" storytellers? I wondered at the stories that might have been lived by the women dancing around me at the wedding and what might have happened to their mothers.

A few days later I sent an email to my friends and, trying to duplicate the conditions of my wedding conversation, asked them to write the story of their mothers' lives, just the facts, in 2,000 words or less. "It's not about you," I said. "You're just a footnote in her story." I was looking for stories but also thought this exercise might jumpstart thinking about the fullness of women's lives. Or maybe it could be a sort of sociology experiment demonstrating the commonalities of experience in the mothers of one population group. I confined my test to one occupation, one locale and one gender: actor, Vancouver, female.

It was so simple, like walking across a room. With every step of this journey though, from 2004 to now, the room has become larger. Much, much larger.

Imagine you're me, hitting send to a group email, thinking you might hear something back from a few people who had mothers living lives something like your own (we're co-workers remember) but that there might be one story that was a bit different. Then, just 45 minutes later, there was an email from my friend Julia, with a story that took place in Hungary, starting in 1930. There was a travelling circus with a knife-throwing act, a father who disappeared from the Russian army and showed up after the war with amnesia, a midnight escape from the Communists, and then the cold of Winnipeg, where her mother started a new life as a prima ballerina. Not only was this nothing like my mother's life, it was unlike any true story I'd ever read!

Then a letter came from my friend and teacher Micki, whose grandfather was an English baron (really??) who lived as a missionary in Tasmania in 1900 before moving his family, including Micki's mother, to India. Then I got an email from Patti, whose mother grew up in Vancouver and sang and danced as she sold war bonds, looking every bit the social success—to those who did not know that

Patti's grandmother was creating mayhem for her family because of undiagnosed bipolar disorder. I thought I knew these people!

More and more stories arrived as my email was forwarded again and again.

Years ago, I asked an acting teacher how we could possibly play women from history. "How did they even think about their lives?" "Exactly like us," she answered. I didn't believe her. I was modern, educated and connected. I had big thoughts, I talked about big ideas. It was obvious to me that most women in the past were largely silent and had small lives, small thoughts. They probably didn't even know how to think; they weren't allowed to think. The stories flooding my inbox proved my assumptions wrong. There was life out there!

I should say here that every story I received that followed the template I sent out was as compelling, unique and interesting as the story I heard at the wedding. At first, I thought maybe I just had some very talented friends with amazing mothers. But not all my friends are writers, and many would describe their mothers as ordinary. Some of the people who sent me stories had strange concepts of punctuation, grammar and spelling; they wrote their stories as poems or letters; they asked questions and quoted conversations. However, if they told the facts of their mothers' lives in chronological order, kept themselves out of the way as much as possible (including their opinions), it was possible to see the woman they wrote of, to feel her wonder and sorrow and to witness her bravery. Each life was tracked through the circumstances of family, religion and politics, giving the heroine dignity, purpose and a great story, whether she was a "good mother" or not.

These were the stories of women I had hoped to find—and they were everywhere!

I should also say that the stories that didn't follow the template were often incomprehensible or incomplete. Many in this category told a story about their mother rather than their mother's story. Or told a story about the writer with her mother as a supporting character, or about her dad, or about the town they lived in.

Then there were stories that rambled through variations of "My mother was such a loving woman, she had a hard life and I really love her," and not much more. This is the description of an icon, not a person. It's also self-focused, a declaration that emphasizes the love and guilt of the speaker more than the qualities of the woman who is or was their mom. It's the voice heard everywhere near Mother's Day, choked with emotion, extolling the virtues of the women who give everything and love unconditionally. As an actor, believe me, it's boring to play an icon. As a person, it's impossible to live as one. We all fail.

It was only while getting these writers back on track that I realized how necessary and uncommon it was to separate the facts of our mothers' lives from how we feel about them. The bonding between a mother and child is primordial, the lifeblood of survival before we are conscious enough to know what survival means. In the moment of birth, most parents understand the profound obligation they have taken on for the sake of another. Yes, there is often sacrifice, heartache and great love that is sometimes unappreciated, but it's not universal. Not everyone who gives birth bonds with their child; not everyone who feels the deep love for another or takes on the full extent of caring for another has given birth. And yet the facts of individual lives are so obscured by the size of these emotions that most women in history have not been described in any way except "Mother."

Along the journey of this project, I've also witnessed how hurtful this Mother's Day voice is to those who lost their mothers at a young age, had a terrible mother, have not birthed or adopted children, or who have but feel they are failing at the whole mothering thing. These people feel excluded from a conversation that says worthy women can only be one thing—perfect love. The writing template I sent out sidestepped this emotional minefield by asking people to look at the facts of their mothers' lives and record them without judgement.

More and more stories came in. Together, they told of women's history around the world and throughout the 20th century, the stories behind the headlines: stories of wealth, poverty, accomplishments, despair, addictions, adoptions, tragedies and weird twists of fate. It was humbling to read the candour with which the writers wrote.

One of the many hidden bonuses was the relief writers found in an assignment that asked them to write the intimate details of a life so close to their own without the clutter of personal feelings, opinions and judgements. "It's not about you!" Many used this assignment as an excuse to contact distant relatives or once close friends of their mothers to verify facts or hear more stories. Immediate families compared notes on shared childhoods, exploring very different perceptions of the same people and events. Rifts, misunderstandings and buried but not forgotten sorrows were given voice, and many were healed. And, of course, many mothers marvelled at how their lives were expressed by children they assumed hadn't been paying attention.

After a few months, we started meeting to share our wealth. Greedy for more, I hoped those still hesitant might be encouraged to write after hearing the stories of others. It worked.

What other forum encourages people to share these details?

People found hidden connections. In our initial group of about 50, we discovered there were two women whose mothers were schizophrenic, two whose mothers had died when their daughters were 10, and two whose alcoholic mothers couldn't stop drinking until they died. After feeling so alone all their lives, these women found someone in their own social group who understood some of their pain.

Someone would say "Well, my mom was just a mom," and then read a story that broke your heart. We take so much for granted. It got so we would all smile in anticipation when a newcomer said their mom didn't have much of a story: "She doesn't know what she's got!" After living our lives in constant comparison to others, judging and conforming, it was thrilling to celebrate the unique aspects of women's lives and just wonder, "How did she cope?"

When a story did seem flat, there were always questions to ask about what was going on beneath the surface, about how this mother and her circumstances were unique. I would say, "there's no shame in the facts" but it was interesting to see how shame takes cover beneath a need for conformity. Some people go to great lengths to avoid talking about... well that's the point, isn't it? Often people didn't have any idea what they were hiding or if anything should be hidden. All they knew was that people didn't talk about their mothers, and that meant women's stories stayed hidden too.

Although it was often tempting, we made a point to stay away from trying to figure out what might be wrong with either the mom or the writer. This desire to fix or judge is the basis of most conversations about mothers, and it quickly became apparent how dull and generic those types of conversations are.

Instead, we discussed these stories as works of art—like plays, an approach the actors (who were also now writers) understood. Our focus was the coherence of the story rather than the quality of the writing or judgements about the characters. Discussions centred around moments when a mother made choices—for a husband, a job, an escape. How many options did she think she had? We marvelled at how women coped, wondered whether a smothering mother was better than a distant one, and discussed how women lived in other countries, other cultures and different eras. In these meetings, we bore witness to someone bearing witness to the struggles and joys of a woman we didn't know but who now felt like a member of our family.

It was surprising to see how this simple act of witnessing created empathy and connection even between strangers. Regardless of our backgrounds or cultures, we became daughters together.

Being actors, we saw the potential for telling these incredible stories on stage. Jenn Griffin, one of the daughters and a playwright and poet, merged many stories together like a tapestry into different shows that told six, 10, 15 and 20 stories at a time. In 2008, we formed a non-profit society and published an anthology of 31 mother stories.

That was just the beginning.

Part VII
SAMPLE STORIES

ONE OF THE MOST ENJOYABLE ASPECTS OF THIS PROJECT IS HEARING OTHER PEOPLE'S STORIES. SOME FIND THIS HARD TO BELIEVE, BEING SO CAUGHT UP IN THEIR OWN LIVES AND WHAT THEY'LL SAY ABOUT THEIR MOTHER. BEING A WITNESS TO SOMEONE ELSE'S MOTHER IS WHEN "IT'S NOT ABOUT YOU" TAKES ON A WHOLE NEW MEANING.

In the following stories three different mothers and their daughters deal with particular challenges, the mothers in how to live them, the daughters in how to record them. They're each 2000 words long. You can see that a lot of story can fit in 2000 words. Each of the writers have written a preamble stating how they came to hear of the project, their experience while writing, and what the impact of having written and shared their stories has meant to them. In addition I have written a few words of introduction for each.

150

ANDREA FECKO

We ran a campaign for stories in the community of North Vancouver in preparation for a play we were commissioned to create at Presentation House Theatre. I talked to people and put up posters in churches, community centres, libraries, women's centres, food banks and anywhere else people congregated offering free workshops. Many people were too busy, too distracted, or suspicious of someone wanting to know about their mother. However a nurse working at the Palliative Care center of the local hospital had seen one of our shows and, wanting to write about her mother, put up a sign-up sheet in the staff room asking for others interested to join her for a workshop. Eight women – nurses, volunteers and friends and family of them—enlisted. Andrea Fecko was one of these women.

As you will see her mother's story is filled with many dramatic events, rich with details and dialogue because that's how Andrea's mother told these stories to her as they worked and waited in South Africa for their husband and father to come home. In editing her story, we worked on making the City of Prague more of a central character, the fantasy place they were exiled from. Andrea's dilemma in writing was to choose which of her mother's many stories to record. She also had to fill in the gaps of her mother's later years when stories weren't told as often.

I heard about this project when I was a volunteer in the palliative program on the North Shore. It was offered to us as a workshop we could attend.

It immediately was of interest to me as my mother was a good story teller and her story was very vivid in my mind and I wanted to share it with my children.

Marilyn was our mentor/guide and avid listener and gave us very useful guidelines as to how to organize our stories and helped us edit them. My story seemed to flow out of me but I did need guidance in cutting out the superfluous and unnecessary words. I did not expect to be as moved emotionally as I was when I read it to others, and that took me completely by surprise. I was also so pleased that I could give my children and grandchildren this legacy.

Because of the impact it had on me I was moved to encourage seven friends to also write the stories of their mothers with the help of Marilyn, and the effect on all of them was profound. They discovered, as had I, their mothers as people apart from themselves, with their humanity, history, difficulties and joys. We were all inspired and came away with perhaps more love and understanding of our mothers and how they had shaped our lives and our histories.

This experience has really encouraged me to keep on writing and sharing with my children and at the same time always gives me food for thought.

My mother's story: Eliska Kadlecova

In the 1920's, every Sunday, Eliska Kadlecova, her brothers and sister would take walks with their father through the streets of Prague. He was an engineer and taught them the history of the buildings, the architectural styles, and the myths that make Prague what it is. Eli, my mother, loved her city and thought she would never leave.

Eli was born on the 6th January 1916, the Feast of the Three Kings–The Epiphany. It was a time when Prague was in the midst of the First World War and it was also the end of the Austro-Hungarian Empire.

Her father was in charge of building factories for the production of sugar country wide. Her mother stayed at home with Eli, her brother, Venda, who was four years older, her brother Mila, who was six years younger, and Olga, who was born in 1924.

They lived in a big apartment, above her grandparent's hospoda called the "Red Mill" which was central to their lives. It was a glorious childhood and Eli was bright, beautiful, funny, and beloved.

Their grandmother particularly adored Venda and Eli. Their grandfather sat at a table allocated to him in the restaurant. He had a moustache that twirled at the ends and always wore a watch on a chain. The children accompanied him, in a horse drawn carriage, to collect rents at properties they owned. They also loved feeding the horses that brought the beer barrels. On a hot day my grandmother, who loved the peace of Sunday, would sit on the balcony, with her feet in a basin of cold water, books at her side and eat ice cream from a big bowl.

Eli was full of mischief. Being the oldest sister, she was often required to look after her younger brother and sister. When she took them to the park, she would sometimes ask the park attendant to keep an eye on them whilst she went on a date. After a few hours she would pick them up on her way back. Once, when she had not completed a dress making assignment, she asked a friend if she could use hers. Eli got an A for the project and the friend got a C.

For Christmas they had a traditional Czech menu. They fattened two geese on the balcony: one for the family, and one for the customers of the pub, who could not afford a good dinner. There were also carp in a basin filled with water. These were respectively butchered and bonked on the head by the cook, and were one of the reasons Eli was never squeamish when it came to catching fish or skinning animals.

Eli spent a lot of time in her grandmother's hospoda doing whatever chores were necessary. She was a favorite with the customers and loved being there.

Her brother Mila, a beautiful boy, was favoured by his father because of his love and talent for all things technical. He was also full of mischief and would give his friends boxing lessons if they would do his homework.

Life changed dramatically in 1930 when one day Mila, calling out to a friend as he crossed the road, did not see the truck that killed him instantly. Eli's mother's hair turned grey overnight and her father was never the same. The family moved to a villa in the suburbs, needing to be somewhere without reminders of Mila at every turn.

As a young woman Eli had many suitors. She attended balls and afternoon dance teas, always with a sense of fashion and style. She attended a school for home economics and was a most gifted chef, artist, and needlewoman.

At the age of 23 she met her first husband Dr. Vaclav Skakal. He was a doctor of law and a member of Prague's high society. They were married in 1939 just as the war was beginning. They lived in his mansion and had a fulltime housekeeper and chauffer. Eli had all her clothes tailor made, including her shoes, belts and gloves. Artists, judges, politicians, and musicians were their company. They had no children.

As World War Two progressed the parties continued with even more abandon as no one knew what the next day might hold. Czechoslovakia was occupied by German forces. Sometimes German Officers would move into their house. My mother told me of standing beside a woman holding her baby, watching the Germans leave, and a soldier came and bayoneted the baby. It was an awful time.

When the war ended, there was much celebration. The trials of the war had solidified the identity of the Czech people. Men, who had escaped Czechoslovakia to join the Czech Free Forces in France and England, returned and were feted by their compatriots for their patriotism and heroism. Life found a semblance of normalcy.

In 1946 my mother went to an afternoon tea dance with a girlfriend. A man asked her to dance. He told her he would marry her, and that he had danced with her many years before. She did not remember this and protested that she was married. He said it did not matter and made a date with her. She did not keep the date. A few weeks later she was getting off a tram in downtown Prague and there he was, changing a flat tire on his car.

As soon as he saw her, he came to her and said "We had a date—now don't move, you are coming with me". And so started the romance and the love affair. Eventually he went to visit Dr. Skakal and said he wanted him to divorce his wife as he wanted to marry her. Dr. Skakal called him a thin toothed snake and dared him to find a lawyer who would handle the case. He found a lawyer and the divorce went through. His name was Josef Baus, known as Pepa.

My father, an engineer, had worked in India, Persia, and was now posted to South Africa for three years. This was darkest Africa as far as my mother was concerned, and the end of the earth, but she was prepared to go as she knew they would return in three years. My father left for South Africa and my mother joined him there in November 1947. Before she left, her father insisted she take all her jewelry, sewing it into her clothes, hiding more in the toothpaste. She remembered sitting with him at the airport and him taking his leave of her with such sadness. She didn't know that he had terminal lung cancer and hadn't told her so she would not change her plans.

The flight to South Africa took three days, with over night stops in Amsterdam and Nairobi. Finally on the 10th November she arrived in Johannesburg and they were married on the 15th. Unfortunately, just before Christmas, when she was six weeks pregnant with me, she received a telegram with news that her father had died. She was in a foreign place, Christmas in the heat instead of the snow, with no friends or family. Homesickness overtook her.

They lived in a company house, met the few Czech families there and made some South African friends. My parents bought shares in a Czech company that designed and manufactured clothes. I was born in August 1948 and their love was complete: my father was 45 and my mother was 32.

In 1950 my father was called back to Prague for a conference. The Communists had nationalized his company but he believed his job was secure. When he arrived his passport was taken and he was told to ask us to return. He had been in the Czech Free Forces and many of his comrades in arms were now imprisoned by the Communists, so my father now knew he wasn't safe. He got word through a Czech consul to my mother telling her to stay put. My mother, whose English was still very limited, was left with me in a house that the company would no longer pay for, not knowing if and when my father would return.

A Czech family heard of our plight and took us to live with them. Because my mother was a competent seamstress she got a job in the factory she had shares in and would leave me with the family during the day and go to work. She would go early in the morning by train, surrounded by Africans, which for her was very new, and come home quite late at night.

Six months later. After escaping in the dead of night over a river into Austria, my father returned to us with nothing more than a valise. My parents sold my mother's jewelry and with the proceeds, put a deposit on a house. They bought a second hand bed and couch and a lovely oil painting, that I still own. The bed stands were tomato boxes and they sat on these to toast the oil painting.

My father found work, and my mother continued working as a seamstress so she could stay at home with me and bring in some income. They were immigrants in a time when there was no help for immigrants, and yet they did the best they could and enjoyed life at every opportunity.

Our house was always perfectly kept and flowers from her garden always adorned the table. My mother would go for walks and gather cuttings from other gardens as she went.

Life was good. Every day, before my father came home, my mother would brush her hair and put on lipstick in order to greet him. Dinner was always a three course affair of her excellent cooking. In the evening they would sit together, my father playing patience and my mother sewing hems or beading. They would listen to the radio and at 7pm my father would make tea.

Every Monday evening they would go to the movies; she loved them, and the theatre. She also loved to read all the gossip magazines—mostly to see what everyone was wearing. Friday nights were spent playing canasta with Czech friends, the Borgens. They alternated between houses, and as the Borgens arrived Steve would kiss my mother's hand and my father would kiss Lilly's hand.

My mother had a sparkling voice. She would sing to me at night, and when we travelled the first thing she asked, as we set upon our journey, was "what song should we sing?" They were always Czech songs.

There were picnics and gatherings, food and baking. My parent's love endured and my father would say that he always loved her ringing laughter. She remained funny, elegant and graceful.

In October 1968 my mother and I were finally able to visit Prague. It was just as beautiful as she had described to me. But then the Russians invaded and we had to sneak onto a bus of foreign geologists to escape the country. She loved Prague but again couldn't stay.

My father, died in 1978, at the age of 74. My mother did not break; she did not crumble, but she never ever looked at or considered another man, although they did look at and consider her.

In 1980 my husband, daughter and I moved to North Vancouver. As I would not move without her, in 1981 she immigrated, once again, to Canada. Here she continued being a devoted grandmother, mother and friend. She was always gracious and yet held her own opinion.

Towards the end she was depressed, arthritic, and had senile dementia. She refused a hip operation and my daughter remembers visiting her in the care home. My mother gyrated her hips making them click, saying "Listen – castanets".

She died in 1999. Her ashes are now in Prague, with my father's. I took them there, mixed them with potting soil and dug them into the Czech earth. She would have approved.

••

WRITING MY MOTHER'S STORY: LISA BUNTING

Lisa and I knew each other for years as actors and neighbours but I never knew anything about her mother. When Lisa told me what she went through to write and the impact on her life since writing about her mother, I glimpsed some of the power available to people through this process. Lisa has participated in some shows and a workshop on her story but the core of it remains very much as first splatted on the page.

When Marilyn first invited me as one of her female actor friends to write my mother's story, I instantly knew that I would, that I had to and it was as though I had just been waiting for someone to ask.

The actual writing was harder than I imagined. I have an ambivalent relationship with my mother, whom I love dearly but whose mental illness had occupied my adolescence and been one of the sources of the PTSD which I had suffered and survived.

When I first attempted to commit my mother's story to paper, just the facts, ma'am, in two thousand words, I experienced free-floating, paralyzing rage. At what, I wasn't sure. Anger at Marilyn for forcing me to do it? Anger that my mother had fallen through the cracks of our society? Shame that I'd failed to save her? Anger that I had to admit to my failure?

In order to meet the deadline and keep myself out of it factually and emotionally, I wrote Mom's story in the third person, as though I were her biographer. It was a physical relief to get the words onto the page. I felt lighter, detached, compassionate, forgiving of myself and her and triumphant that I had channeled the anger I'd felt and emerged with something that suggested as much between the lines as was on the page.

It was a powerful experience getting to read it out loud for the first time amongst a group of more than a dozen women, some of whom had already read their stories and others who were reading for the first time. Each daughter invariably stumbled on one moment during the course of her reading, and was always surprised at the moment by which she'd been caught.

Eventually, I was able to rewrite the story in first person. I have grown with the project over the years, using fragments collaged into the larger kaleidoscope that is the My Mother's Story staged readings, finalizing a draft for the original MMS book, and now, looking at my mother's story again before its inclusion in this book. I even told Mom's story once in a workshop using a clothesline, graciously held by two other daughters, as I clothes-pegged props along it, story-telling the whole way.

I would say that writing my mother's story got it out of the dark pockets where it was hiding in my body and into the light, where I've been able to make peace with its many facets over time.

BODIL BUNTING

Bodil Ingegerd Malmström is born in Malmö, Sweden on January 25, 1930, the second of four daughters for Ture, a clothing merchant, and his wife, Elsa. Growing up, there's lots of laughter in the home, but Ture has a temper and the girls dread their father's unpredictable bursts of rage. Bodil considers herself a black sheep. She smiles with closed lips, hiding her poor teeth. She is academically weak but intuitive like her mother, a natural mimic and class clown. During World War II, when Sweden is neutral, the sisters are evacuated to the country.

An avid theatre-goer, Bodil waits at stage doors for autographs. She dreams of being a nurse but following high school attends secretarial school, then works in her brother-in-law's office until his early death. She goes to the Sorbonne in Paris, studies French, then works as an au pair for families in France and England.

In 1955, fluent in three languages, she becomes a tour-guide with Lignebus, travelling around

Europe. Once, when a tourist asks about an approaching town's industry, she answers "steel" just as the bus rises to reveal multiple windmills.

One evening at the American Club in Nice, a young man asks her to dance. "I'm waiting for friends," she replies. "Well, you can dance while you're waiting, can't you?" She looks around and, deciding that he has the safest face in the establishment, agrees. The following morning, he joins her and her friends at the beach. His name is John Pearce Bunting, a Canadian touring Europe following his graduation from McGill with a business degree. To the delight of her passengers, he follows her tour bus in his rented blue sports car until she agrees to come to Canada and marry him.

In Forest Hill, Toronto, Bodil is welcomed into the Dunvegan Road home of her future parents-in-law, Harriet and Alfred. Family and friends "swoon" at the romantic notion of Pearce having captured the heart of this "exotic", vivacious, yet shy Swede.

In June of 1956, Canadian relatives fly in for the occasion of Bodil and Pearce's wedding in St. Peter's Church in Malmö. Photos in Swedish society pages show her Grace Kelly-like in a three-pointed crown, veil and white gown, carrying a large spray of lilies; Pearce is fresh-faced with slicked-back hair, a tuxedo and white handkerchief. Years later, Mom remembers feeling uncomfortable and resentful in her older sister's hand-me-down dress. Dad says he knew he was making a mistake even as he walked down the aisle.

She wants to be a stewardess but Pearce says no. Joining him on a business trip to New York, she is selected out of Art Linklater's studio audience. Telling her she looks like Kim Novak, she is insulted.

In 1957, Pearce and Bodil move into an apartment duplex on Burnaby Boulevard. In

September, their first child, Elsa Brenda, is born. Studio portraits suggest a tender mother-daughter bond, Bodil's shoulders rounded from nursing, back swayed from lifting, her face dewy and soft.

Bodil works hard to fit in to Canadian culture, Toronto society and the expectations of her North Toronto family. She does not want to be perceived as "a little immigrant" and is self-conscious about her accent. She regrets leaving the house to get to a party on time, the wails of her nursing child fading as breast milk seeps into her evening dress. One afternoon, feeling unwell, at the advice of a neighbour she cancels a planned luncheon and has a miscarriage.

She volunteers for and attends events at the National Ballet of Canada and Art Gallery of Ontario. In a photo taken at the Cinderella Ball, she crosses her fingers as a footman helps her try on a glass slipper; in a photo from 1969, she is Mrs. Robinson to her husband's Benjamin Braddock.

In March of 1960, Harriet Elizabeth (Lisa) is born and Mark Alfred in May of 1962.

The family moves to a brick home with a mature garden on Dinnick Crescent. Bodil becomes an excellent stockbroker's wife, hostess and cook. She is stylish and tasteful, flirtatious and bawdy. She gets laughs at cocktail parties with apparently ingenuous malapropisms like "croin" (crotch and groin). To a group of women admiring her newborn son in his crib, she remarks, "He's very well hung, isn't he?"

She later says the early years of raising her children are the happiest of her life. She travels with Pearce on business trips to Peru, Mexico, Japan and China. The family attends Expo '67, skis at Osler Bluff and summers on Logan Lake, where mothers laughingly swap brown paper packages hiding books with titles such as The Sensuous Woman and dads arrive on weekends with fresh supplies of groceries, liquor, and guests. Fathers and sons troll by in their outboards, hoping for a glimpse of the Swedish "babe" in her bathing suit.

In 1969, Pearce returns from a business trip to Thailand with an STD. Bodil is devastated. She throws him a 40th birthday party under a tent in the backyard.

In 1972, the family moves to a bigger house on Daneswood Avenue.

In the spring of 1973, Bodil finds a Don Mills gas station receipt in Pearce's jacket pocket. Wondering what business he might have north of the city limits, she confronts him and he admits to having an affair with a secretary. She tells him she is taking the children to Europe for the summer while he sorts himself out.

In what she later called Pearce's "Summer of Turmoil", Bodil rents a car and drives her children through France's Loire Valley and to visit her youngest sister in Nyon, Switzerland.

That fall, after making love the night before, Bodil awakens to find Pearce gazing down at her. "You look like an angel when you're sleeping," he says. He leaves on a week-long business trip and, on his return, checks into an airport hotel.

On a late Sunday afternoon in October, Pearce comes to the house. A first and last family meeting is called to tell the children he's leaving.

For the next year Bodil remains behind the bedroom door or emerges with red-rimmed eyes to pace the first-floor hallway. Arms crossed and talking to herself, she wears a visible tread in the carpet awaiting her husband's return. She is unaware that he has met someone at a summer wedding, who later becomes his wife and the mother of two more children.

On a winter morning in 1974, her daughters find her in her bedroom, frozen, unblinking and holding up three fingers. They drive her to Sunnybrook Hospital's emergency room in her nightie, coat and slippers, where she is admitted to the psychiatric ward. Stabilized on medication, two months later she is released.

1974-1989: A succession of hospital admissions, psychiatrists, diagnoses and medications. She falls in love with doctors and resents the antipsychotics which cause weight gain, dry mouth, trembling. They make her feel "numb", "evened out", and unable to access her anger. Now in her forties, she has two colon cancer surgeries requiring that she wean off medication. After the second surgery, she refuses to go back on.

In 1976, following three years of separation, the divorce is finalized. Bodil moves to a townhome on Keewatin Avenue. She dates various men, including Sam, a married Sunnybrook psychiatric nurse. He attends Bunting family therapy sessions wearing a jade ring given to her by her ex-husband. Her daughters arrive home from school to find him trying to persuade Bodil to turn the townhouse into a group home. Suspicious of her neighbour, Joe, Bodil passes him on the front walk saying, "I like your cocksucker suit." She sprinkles baby powder on the floor of the basement laundry room to track footprints of omnipresent intruders. She gets messages from license plates and sees familiar faces in traffic. She follows a funeral procession in her car to Mississauga, wearing a top hat and laughing hysterically.

In 1979, her father, Ture, dies in Sweden. She does not attend his funeral.

In January of 1987, Brenda gives birth prematurely to Bodil's first granddaughter, Zoe, who has cerebral palsy.

In 1989, Bodil moves to a duplex on Castlefield Avenue. For a time, Brenda and Zoe live in the basement suite. She takes courses, works and volunteers in the community, mostly with social services. She has a business card printed: "Bodil Bunting, Mental Health Counselor".

At Christmas, Bodil flies to Sweden with Mark. She disappears in the Copenhagen airport and is found, three days later, in a Danish airport hotel room where she's been sitting staring at a wall. She is brought to Sweden, where her mother, Elsa, begs not to be left alone with her.

In 1991, Lisa moves to Vancouver. Elsa dies. Bodil does not attend the funeral but flies her daughters there.

On her "six-ta-ti-sixth" birthday, January 25, 1996, Bodil's second granddaughter, Sofia, is born.

She moves into a room at the YWCA on Woodlawn Avenue. She meets granddaughter "Fia" for the first time on a park bench at the end of the street. She is asked to leave the Y for allegedly hitting another resident.

A real estate agent comes to the door and talks her into selling her Castlefield home. Her sister-in-law takes her in.

Friends help her rent a condo in their building on Albany Ave. She moves out shortly afterwards, believing they are following her everywhere, persecuting her through the walls.

She is moved by family to an apartment in a seniors building on Merton Street, where Pearce pays the rent directly. Brenda and Mark strategize an intervention by a psychogeriatric team; Bodil humours them by inviting them all for lunch, then throwing them out.

In December of 1999, Bodil's third granddaughter, Mark's daughter, Eve, is born.

She makes it through each sleep-deprived day and night by sheer force of will. When voices trouble her, she walks in the early morning through Mount Pleasant Cemetery. She rarely answers the phone and keeps the blinds shut. She invites only immediate family to visit for two to three hours at a time. She dotes on her granddaughters, Zoe, Sofia and Eve.

She reads biographies, the inspirational writings of Eleanor Roosevelt, Liv Ullmann and

Anna Morrow Lindberg and books on health and nutrition. She copies favourite passages into journals and occasionally keeps her own.

By late 2014, she has shrunken, with long, unwashed hair and missing teeth. She is deaf in one ear and blind in one eye. She plugs the sink with coffee grounds, leaves on appliances, elements and taps, burning food and flooding the bathroom. Her toenails grow out and sideways and curl into the bottoms of her toes. She lives in the dark, eating Tim Horton's coffee, soup and donuts. She will not open the door for Meals on Wheels.

In March of 2015, her children are able to move her to Cedarhurst Dementia Care Centre. She gets a health card, doctors, tests, glasses, dentures, hearing aids, her hair and nails done and three homemade meals a day. She begins to participate in group activities, including singing and dancing.

My mother's story originally ended with the words, "She loves to laugh. She's still in love with Dad. And she talks to walls."

She no longer talks to walls, though as I fed her dinner two nights ago, she was singing a combination of Swedish and gibberish nursery rhymes under her breath. She enjoys bouncing the beachball, getting neck and shoulder massages and sitting in the sunshine, and she gives and receiving kisses, always with a thank you. Since moving to long-term care at Meighen Manor, dementia has swallowed the mental illness, and most of the rest of her. She is distilled to her essence: Now and Love.

• •

WRITING MY MOTHER'S STORY: DOLORES DRAKE

Dolores is one of my actor friends in Vancouver and she will tell you that I pushed her into writing about her mother and I'm so glad I did! When she sent me her story though, I wasn't sure what to do with it.

This was in the early days of the project when people were sending me all kinds of things—from sentence fragments and poems, to emails where their mothers answered questions for them. I wasn't sure if we needed conformity and if so to what. Finally I decided to insist on the parameters of the recipe and, as much as she has written it in dialogue, Dolores' story fits that. We can see her mother in the fragments of images Dolores includes and in the attitudes of other women living in Newfoundland who remain the models for Dolores for who her mother might have been. That's all the information Dolores had to work with. I love this story for how it demonstrates the creativity and licence that can be used to tell a story.

Dolores is also a playwright and has written two plays about her father but felt stymied to write anything about her mother. Her original story was quite short and was about not knowing many facts about her mother despite her best intentions and desires to know more. Dolores participated in many of our theatrical events and workshops and it was through this process that more and more memories came to light which she used to expand her story. So when she says she wrote her story in half an hour, well, that was her discovery draft.

When Marilyn first asked me to write My Mother's Story, I flatly said "I can't do that".

I listened to Marilyn explain the project and thought it sounded wonderful—for other people.

I explained that my mother died when I was 12, and had been sick since I was 8, so there was so much I didn't know about her.

How could I possibly write her story?

"Write about that," Marilyn said.

After much griping and mumbling, I sat down with a notepad one afternoon, and wrote it in about half an hour.

I started with my most visual memory of her (the Hats) and it grew from there.

I was surprised at how much emotion came up as I was writing, and how it made me want to know more about my family and how much I did actually remember. I cried and laughed, and felt connected to my roots and my mother.

In an attempt to find out more, I eventually travelled home to Newfoundland and connected with relatives I didn't know I had. What a gift in my life to reconnect with my homeland and people.

The first reading of all our stories live at the Arts Club on Mother's Day, we were blown away by the audience's reaction. People were so moved and engaged. They laughed, cried and cheered.

I felt the power of truth, of family, of women, of history, women's history, of the extraordinary in the ordinary.

I was so grateful to be a part of it.

Many staged readings later, Mother's Day became a good day for me, one in which I had something to share instead of only feeling alone and sad.

Thank you, Marilyn. Thank you mothers everywhere.

Margerite Turpin

She wore hats, hats with veils, whenever she went to church or visiting neighbours. They made her look mysterious and she was and indeed still is a mystery to me.

Her maiden name was Margerite Turpin.

What comes to me most is how much I don't know, it was all so long ago. I have memories of course, snapshots of memories like pictures of a trip.

I don't know exactly where she was born or exactly where she's buried, nor exactly what she died of.

To understand this you'd have to understand Outport Newfoundlanders. The one thing for certain is Newfoundland is where her story began and ended. She never left the island. Did she want to?

She was born Sept. 1st, 1918.

According to my oldest half-sister Dot, she was born and raised and died in the same town we grew up in – St Lawrence or its sister town Little St Lawrence, Newfoundland.

She was one of nine children, five brothers and three sisters.

"Where was she in this line up, Dot?"

"For Christ's sake, I don't know!" Dot says.

"Did she ever talk about her childhood?"

"Yes likely now, she hardly talked to me at all."

What was she like as a child, a teenager, a young married woman?

I can only speculate and imagine. Outport life before modern conveniences was rough. People worked hard, children too as soon as they were old enough. Expectations, dreams, ambitions were low. Life was about survival. The only expectation was to be tough, stay healthy and earn your keep.

Did she finish school? Unlikely at that time but more likely than the boys. She knew how to read and write. I remember her doodling on notepads, playing with letters, and I have a memory of her teaching me to do this one cold winter night.

She liked to write letters to her sister Gert who lived in New York. Did she wish she had gone with her? Aunt Gert sent us clothes and hats. My mother was the best dressed woman in the cove.

Aunt Mary, my mother's brother's wife, the oldest living member of our family, is 88 and ailing and was never too open with information at the best of times. Older Newfoundlanders are the most present people I've ever met. They rarely indulge in reminiscing the past and the future is no further than Tuesdays bingo game. What she does remember and repeats continually is that my mother was pregnant before she married my father.

Every family in the cove had 9 or 10 children, but apparently no one was having sex. Once I was sent to the store to pick up a box of Blue Biscuits. I found out later that this was the Outport woman's code word for Kotex pads.

So she grew up and married her first husband Gregory Turpin and with him she had 4 children. Dot, Howard, Walter, and Mary. Howard died at 7 months old, got a flu and died. A few years later her husband Gregory was killed in a mine cave in. Dot told me the sirens wailed and everyone waited to see who had lived and who had died.

My mother was alone now with three children. What were her options in a small Newfoundland outport? She could put her children in the orphanage in St. John's and go to work cleaning houses for rich merchants. Aunt Mary and many other women did that. Or she could find another husband and keep her children. That's what she did, she found my father Randall Drake.

"Where did she meet my father, Dot?"

"Oh, at the Club probably, where else?"

My father was a widower raising 6 children on his own, living in the neighbouring town. He needed a wife, so they met and married, the Newfoundland Brady Bunch. There were 9 kids now but only 4 at home.

I was the love child that brought them together. Then she had my two brothers, Sonny and Gary, and never lived to see us grow up.

"What was she really like Dot?" I ask.

"How do you expect me to know what she was like? You knows how distant she was. Didn't talk much unless it was to God."

Oh yes, I remember the rosary beads.

"Was she depressed when she lost the baby?"

"She was always depressed if you ask me, and stressed."

"About what?"

"How the frig should I know?"

I have my few precious snapshot memories… Her getting dressed to go to the club with my Dad, doing my hair for church, teaching me to write sitting at our old kitchen table, doing the wash with the old wringer washer, saying the rosary at the kitchen window, waiting for my father to get back from fishing at sea. And kicking me outside when the other women were visiting.

Once I came home from school with swollen red hands. I had gotten the strap from Sister David for something or other.

"Mom, Mom, look what she did!" I cried.

She pushed her hair out of her eyes, spreading flour across her forehead.

"Well, you must have done something wrong, she's a nun after all."

I remember her coming to school for Parents Day, when I was in Grade 4, on the wrong day, and the teacher inviting her to stay. There she sat in her hat and veil, while I had to do a speech. I was so embarrassed. She smiled and nodded through the whole thing.

I remember her trying to get a bumblebee out of the back porch with a broom, on the day my older half-brother Jim was shot. Walter came running in the house yelling "Jim's dead, Jim's dead!"

"What's wrong with you Walter," she said, "Don't be so foolish."

And I remember the awful scream that came out of her when she realized he was telling the truth.

It was an accident, the boys firing at cans on a fence with a sawed off shotgun, and Jim deciding to twirl the gun like in the western movies.

And I remember her cleaning the house from top to bottom to get ready for the wake.

The last time I saw her she was lying in a hospital bed crying while I was showing her my new dress. I think she knew she wasn't going to make it. Only 49 she was when we put her in the ground. I was 12.

I'm tempted to fill in the blanks, to make up all the stuff I don't know, to make some sense, to give her life more meaning. I have so often thought about her and missed her because I never really got to know her. I missed her when she was alive....

Of all that was said and unsaid I think she was a lady... a lady who did all the right things and maybe didn't understand why that didn't bring happiness. A gentle, sensitive woman who lived her short life in a very harsh environment.

There are moments I can hear her voice:

"Put your sweater on now, you don't want to catch a chill.

Mind your manners.

Go on and play outside.

Be good..."

• •

There's a story behind everything. How a picture got on a wall. How a scar got on your face. Sometimes the stories are simple, and sometimes they are hard and heartbreaking. But behind all your stories is your mother's story. Hers is where yours began.

Mitch Albom, *For One More Day*

Part VIII

DOING MORE

SOME PEOPLE WANT TO MAKE SURE OF ALL THEIR FACTS BEFORE THEY START TO WRITE; OTHERS WRITE WHAT THEY KNOW FIRST AND THEN VERIFY LATER. IT'S UP TO YOU. WHAT DO YOU NEED TO KNOW?

The detective work of tracking down dates, facts and photos can be quite compelling as thousands of genealogists can attest. Check out your local library for their resources, whether in their catalogues or online. Most librarians love this kind of challenge and can point you in many directions.

Many cities and countries also have societies that maintain the history of almost every ethnic and religious group in their communities. Asking for information here might put you in touch with relatives you never knew or people with whom you can share stories of the immigration and diaspora of your people around the world.

Online there is a wealth of knowledge available, whether through free sites like the LDS website (Church of Latter Day Saints—the Mormons have one of the largest collections in the world of church records from all denominations giving dates of births, deaths, marriages, ship's registries and enrollment in the armed services as well as photos of gravestones) or subscription sites like Ancestry.com that have saved newspaper articles and photos as well as much of the information saved by LDS. They also have an online community where you can attach your family tree to others being created around the world.

In official records you'll find names and dates but also witness the lack of details about many women's lives. Daughters names are regularly forgotten especially if they never married and cross cultural and bi-racial marriages rarely received notice other than condemnation. This is one of the reasons this project exists—to record these details before they're lost.

The best course of action to find details about your mother is to strike out and find the people you used to know and ask them. It's surprising to find out how much people want to connect about a shared past. There may be a relative who has saved all the letters and photos of the larger family and will be a wealth of knowledge. Neighbours might have photos and stories of their families in which your family is also included. School friends of your mother will tell you stories you've never heard before. Your assignment to write this story will open doors all over the world. You are, after all, the best person to tell her story.

The internet is so handy. Many people have found relatives and neighbours on Facebook. Google and LinkedIn might also give links to their children. Inquiries lead to chats and then sometimes visits. You can find the address and often a website for schools, hospitals and prisons your mother may have attended or visited. As her child you can get her health records sent to you to verify details. Adoption papers are often available now for scrutiny. You can use your computer to look up phone numbers all over the world and call them. What will you discover?

Mothership Stories Society,

the non-profit society that directs and guides all aspects of My Mother's Story, was founded in 2008 with the mandate to encourage the writing, collecting and performing of family stories. It is the publisher of the My Mother's Story books, manages commissions and production of My Mother's Story theatrical events, and holds the copyright to all stories and images submitted to our Archive.

We hold that the process of writing and telling the stories of our mothers to be our main product. Other intangible products include an empathy effect that dissolves cultural silos in communities and leads to stronger community bonds, the advancement of skills in effective storytelling, increasing the worldwide resources of women's history and providing the means whereby the disenfranchised find a voice.

Everyone has a mother and every mother has a story. These stories and the curriculum we create facilitate a change in people's understanding of mothers and the place of women in history.

All stories are freely donated to our archive demonstrating our tenet that no story is more valuable than another. The stories featured in our books are also available online in our Archive making our products and the process of writing inclusive to everyone. The value of the Archive is in its diversity of stories and we make concerted efforts to reach and include stories from all aspects of society, all societies. We seek out donations, grants and partnerships that will allow us to increase our outreach and gain the wider support of corporate, public and private sponsors to remove any economic barriers to participation. If you'd like to get involved, bring a workshop to your community, or just learn more, please visit www.mymothersstory.org.

Special Thanks

This book has grown and been filtered through the shared experience and stories of hundreds of women and men. When I asked actors in Vancouver, some of whom were friends, some of whom became friends, to write about their mothers none of us realized we would become Daughters together. Their courage and trust inspired everything that has followed here. The Mother's Lab in North Vancouver continued that shared trust and community as we questioned and experimented with how to talk about our mothers. Andrea Fecko, Michelle Hohn, Sharon Quirt, Pat White, Allesandro Olmedo, and Colleen Rhodes are all ambassadors to this cause. The people who attended workshops at Unity of Vancouver also provided great insights and candor. Likewise special thanks to Leanne and Bob Hume who have spread the word throughout the world on their travels with international schools. Thank you Kimiko Suzuki for opening the door to stories in Japan.

Lori Bamber, a fabulous editor, and Karin Konoval, an insightful writer and friend have given extraordinary direction and encouragement to this book. Visnja Milidragovic, your friendship, passion and grit have pushed this whole project forward page by page. May the gods heap rewards on you all.

I would also like to thank the Mothership boards past and present who kept on me to get this book written: Stephanie Koonar, Romney Grant, Lisa Bunting, Jennifer Molton, Grace Gordon Collins, Mary Charleson, Nancy Bradshaw, Bruce Halliwell, Beverley Boiserry, Craig Goodmurphy and Joan MacLean, our sustaining strength from the beginning.

Thank you Nadine Pedersen for your seeds of inspiration, Jenn Griffin for bringing the mothers to the stage in all incarnations, and to Jenny Arntzen who is taking us forward.

Notes

CPSIA information can be obtained
at www.ICGtesting.com
Printed in the USA
LVHW021100061218
599399LV00003B/3/P